The House from Hell

The True Story of Gertrude Baniszewski One of America's Most Notorious Torture Mom

True Crime Explicit Volume 5

(Second Edition)

Genoveva Ortiz, True Crime Seven

TRUE CRIME 7

Copyright © 2024 by Sea Vision Publishing, LLC

All Rights Reserved.

No part of this publication may be reproduced, distributed, or transmitted in any form or by any means, including photocopying, recording, electronic or mechanical methods, without the prior written permission of the publisher, except in the case of brief quotations embodied in critical reviews and certain other non-commercial uses permitted by copyright law.

Much research, from a variety of sources, has gone into the compilation of this material. We strive to keep the information up-to-date to the best knowledge of the author and publisher; the materials contained herein is factually correct. Neither the publisher nor author will be held responsible for any inaccuracies. This publication is produced solely for informational purposes, and it is not intended to hurt or defame anyone involved.

ISBN: 9798408837533

Table of Contents

Introduction *11*

I The Odd One Out *13*

II An Unhappy Union *17*

III Unlucky in Love *21*

IV The Angry Young Lover *26*

V Two Wayward Girls *31*

VI The Bad Times Begin *38*

VII A Jealous Rage *45*

VIII Back to School *51*

IX The Ringleader *60*

X A Thread of Hope *71*

XI More Missed Opportunities *81*

XII The Basement *88*

XIII The Tattoo *99*

XIV The End Comes *110*

XV A Shocking Scene *122*

XVI The Truth Comes Out *133*

XVII The Truth Comes Out *140*

Conclusion *153*

References *159*

Acknowledgements *161*

I The Abduction *165*

About True Crime Seven *177*

Explore the Stories of
The Murderous Minds

A Note

From True Crime Seven

Hi there!

Thank you so much for picking up our book! Before you continue your exploration into the dark world of killers, we wanted to take a quick moment to explain the purpose of our books.

Our goal is to simply explore and tell the stories of various killers in the world: from unknown murderers to infamous serial killers. Our books are designed to be short and inclusive; we want to tell a good scary true story that anyone can enjoy regardless of their reading level.

That is why you won't see too many fancy words or complicated sentence structures in our books. Also, to prevent typical cut and dry style of true crime books, we try to keep the narrative easy to follow while incorporating fiction style storytelling. As to information, we often find ourselves with too little or too much. So, in terms of research material and content, we always try to include what further helps the story of the killer.

Lastly, we want to acknowledge that, much like history, true crime is a subject that can often be interpreted differently. Depending on the topic and your upbringing, you might agree or disagree with how we present a story. We understand disagreements are inevitable. That is why we added this note so hopefully it can help you better understand our position and goal.

Now without further ado, let the exploration to the dark begin!

Introduction

EVEN NOW, SO MANY DECADES LATER, IT'S difficult for us to wrap our minds around why the Nazis did what they did. The defense they gave at Nuremberg is almost baffling in its simplicity: we were just following orders.

Had millions of Germans just collectively gone insane? How else could so many have accepted the order to carry out those atrocities?

The truth, unfortunately, is that mild-mannered, regular people really made the best Nazis. They obeyed all laws. They didn't question authority. They didn't rock the boat, lest attention be drawn to themselves. After WWI left so many families in a desperate state, it must have been strangely relieving to have a common enemy they could blame their problems on. Perhaps state-sponsored antisemitism provided an acceptable outlet for the darker urges some of them might have been harboring. It certainly helped that Jews had already been a common scapegoat for society's ills and had faced persecution for centuries.

Twenty years after the Nazis were defeated, a similar dynamic was at play at a micro scale in the basement of an Indiana home. We see a woman, Gertrude Baniszewski, filled with hatred after a lifetime of hardship. We also see an innocent teenage girl she blamed all her problems on. Through ways that are still difficult to understand, Gertrude became a ringleader of torture against Sylvia Likens, rallying together a small army of neighborhood children.

But how did she do it? Was it the power of the mob mentality? Were they all jealous of Sylvia? Were they afraid of becoming the odd one out, potentially putting themselves as the second in line for abuse? After all, even Sylvia's innocent little sister ended up partaking in the crimes against her sister.

What causes regular, mild-mannered people to turn into animals?

This book will explore the life of the woman behind one of America's most notorious child abuse cases.

I
The Odd One Out

GERTRUDE VAN FOSSAN WAS BORN AT THE most unlucky time. It was September 22, 1929, and America was just one month into the Great Depression. Her parents, Hugh and Mollie Van Fossan, felt the weight of the greatest recession in the country's history on their shoulders almost immediately. Gertrude was their third child, and soon more were on the way. The family grew to six children, all supported by an increasingly stressed-out father who turned to alcohol for relief.

Resentment became a fixture of young Gertrude's life from the very start. Her mother, for seemingly no apparent reason, held her daughter at arm's length. While she was reportedly warm and loving with the other five children, her third earned her ire. Her coldness towards Gertrude marked the little girl as an outsider, and as a result, her siblings, perhaps following their parent's example, would also come to reject her.

Fortunately, life was not entirely miserable in those early years. Though Gertrude could not win over her mother, her father considered her his favorite child and lavished attention on her. The two were very close, and this relationship created further resentment from Mollie and the other children. Gertrude was both a golden child and the scapegoat of her family all at once.

If Gertrude had known her status as a pariah within her own family, it mattered little to her then. The love from her father was enough for her—but then, tragedy struck, and Gertrude's life would never be the same—or as happy—ever again.

She was eleven years old when one evening, while she practiced her reading, her father abruptly became unwell. Gertrude watched as Hugh gasped for air and rose from his seat only to collapse on the floor beside her. He became motionless and silent. Frightened, she knelt down and begged him to wake up, to no avail.

That was when Mollie rushed in, screaming at the sight of her stricken husband. "What did you do?" she screamed at her terrified daughter. "*What did you do?*"

"I didn't do anything!" Gertrude whimpered. Her mother did not believe her.

Though the family likely would not have been able to afford it, Gertrude asked if she should get the doctor. Her mother informed her that it was too late; her beloved daddy was dead.

Gertrude's happiness crumbled away literally overnight. Witnessing her father's death greatly traumatized her. The memory of it was constantly on her mind, and not even in her sleep was she free from reliving it. She began to suffer from night terrors and on countless nights would wake up screaming. Hugh had been her protector, the one to comfort her when things got scary. Now, all she had was the hostile presence of a family who did not love her.

Her mother grew more resentful of Gertrude since her husband's passing. She blamed her for his heart attack and considered her the cause of all their problems. Though she comforted Gertrude's grieving siblings, she ignored her daughter. When Gertrude's night terrors would wake her, Mollie would become enraged that she was disturbing the sleep of the other children.

Life only grew harder as the years went by. Gertrude's attendance at school became irregular, partly due to the constant bullying she received from her classmates, many of whom were friends with her siblings. Even Mollie took part in the bullying, helping to spread vicious rumors about her daughter being promiscuous and unclean. As a result, Gertrude's relationships with other girls became permanently warped by bitterness, ultimately developing a lifelong hatred for her own gender.

Lacking love at home, Gertrude turned to boys and men as a teenager. The rumors her mother spread now worked in her favor. She had dropped out of school, but boys still came around in the hopes of getting in on the action she was now known for. For Gertrude, her male companions provided not only affection but a means to get away from her home life. In 1945, at sixteen, she met and married an eighteen-year-old police deputy named John Baniszewski.

None of her family attended the wedding.

II
An Unhappy Union

JOHN BANISZEWSKI (PRONOUNCED BAN-I-SHEF-ski) had been looking forward to married life. He had heard all kinds of stories about the things Gertrude was willing to do for a man, and he was happy to have her all to himself. It ended up being quite a shock to him when it became obvious that those rumors were all false.

It turned out that his new bride was not the expert in the bedroom he had expected. In fact, she did not even seem to enjoy having sex in general.

To her, sexual intercourse was a shameful act, something to be endured rather than enjoyed. It was a lesson instilled in her from childhood, thanks to her mother's constant ridicule. Whenever John attempted to become intimate with her, she would acquiesce, though her participation would reportedly end there. She would lie beneath him as still as a corpse, her limbs rigid with discomfort as she waited for him to finish.

To make matters worse, Gertrude lacked the skills of the good homemaker he expected her to be. She had never learned how to cook, and her ability to keep the house clean was subpar. She often suffered from depressive spells that left the house in a filthy state. Still, with nowhere else to go, she was determined to make the marriage work. When she wasn't working as a clerk in drug stores to help make ends meet, she was at home, trying her best to become a better wife.

In time, even sex was no longer as bleak as it had been. Three years into their marriage, Gertrude became pregnant. It was a rare happy time for her, and she devoted herself to making a better home for the baby. These changes initially pleased John, but soon he found himself becoming annoyed with the fact that he was no longer the center of Gertrude's attention.

Their first child, a baby girl named Paula, was born in 1948. Two years later, Gertrude gave birth to Stephanie. Shortly after the arrival of her second child, the stress of her rough upbringing finally caught up to Gertrude, and she experienced a nervous breakdown. She was diagnosed as having "neuroticism," an assessment that would now be considered outdated or defunct. In the current age, psychiatrists would classify her symptoms as a sign of bipolar or borderline personality disorder. Whatever her illness was, it left her constantly tense and emotionally withdrawn from her husband, much to his displeasure.

By all accounts, Gertrude was a good mother during her first marriage. At some point, she realized that John would never exhibit the same sort of warmth and kindness that Hugh had shown her as a child, she could still prove that she was not like Mollie. She devoted all her time and attention to her daughters, who were soon joined by John Jr. (referred to almost exclusively as Johnny in most sources) and another sister, Marie. Having lacked a strong maternal figure in her life, Gertrude learned as much as she could about parenting from doctors and other young mothers, though she made no effort to befriend or get close to other women.

John, on the other hand, was quickly reaching his limit. Gertrude was a disappointment to him. Though she had shown some signs of improving when she first got pregnant, it would amount to very little when it came to his happiness. Being so careful about the children meant that she was more irritating than ever, always nagging him about how much he drank or how much money he spent. When he'd had enough, he began to beat her.

Gertrude had never known what a healthy relationship was supposed to look like. She likely thought that violence was like having sex, just another thing that wives needed to endure from their husbands. It was likely for this reason that she obeyed when John instructed her to hide her bruises whenever she went out, leading to her becoming more reclusive until she figured out how to cover them with makeup. As a policeman, he knew what it could do to his positive reputation if word got out that he battered his wife, and he was an expert in keeping the truth covered up.

It must have come as a relief to him when Gertrude asked him for a divorce in 1955, after ten tedious years together. John accepted, unaware that she would be back again in his life before long.

III

Unlucky in Love

GERTRUDE HAD FOUR CHILDREN, NO MONEY, and no man. She also had a lifelong yearning to be loved. It came as no surprise when only a few months after her divorce from John Baniszewski, she met and married a man named Edward Guthrie during a brief stay in Kansas.

Guthrie was different from John, or so he made it seem. He managed to charm Gertrude right away, allowing her to overlook that he was unemployed and had an even worse problem with alcohol than her ex-husband. Then there was the issue with the children—Guthrie was not a fatherly man; he actively disliked children, though he purposefully did not make that clear to his new wife when it was John's child support payments that were putting food on the table.

Gertrude seemed more than content to make ends meet herself, doing odd jobs such as washing and repairing clothing for neighbors. Child support helped, but those payments were few and far between.

At some point during their short marriage, Guthrie, increasingly tired of having so many children around, hit one of them. It was the start of the splintering of his relationship with his wife. Things grew tense and hostile between them. Once he found a job and was no longer dependent on Gertrude's irregular checks, he filed for divorce, stating in court that his reason for wanting to end the marriage was that he found children annoying.

The divorce was granted easily, putting an end to the union that had lasted less than a year.

Though poor, Gertrude and her children managed to get by on their own for a while. Life was easier without a cruel man wasting away what little money they had on booze; she could not help but feel lonely at times, not to mention the shame she endured for being a single mother in an era when it was still frowned upon. When she ran into her first husband on the street, she jumped at the chance to reconnect with him.

She wanted him around for the sake of the children, but admittedly, she was often feeling rather lonely herself.

Gertrude and John Sr. would marry again, although briefly. The relationship started off on a positive note, with Gertrude doing all she could to keep him happy this time. She was the perfect housewife and mother, and John was quite pleased with the change. In turn, he became kinder and more affectionate towards her.

Unfortunately, a tragedy would soon unravel the newly remarried bliss. Gertrude was pregnant with what was supposed to be her and John's fifth child. Her pregnancy appeared to be going well, with no signs that anything might be wrong. However, Gertrude miscarried for unknown reasons when the baby was nearly full-term.

She'd had miscarriages before, but this one was different. She had gotten so close to being able to hold the infant in her arms, to shower it with love. Her children were her only respite in her difficult life, but this one had been snatched away before it even had the chance to live. It utterly devastated her, and she soon sank into what would be the deepest depression of her life.

Lost in her mourning, she struggled to keep up with the cooking and cleaning, and after a while, she was not able to do them at all. The house grew filthy and the children out of control. John attempted to fix her again through violence, but this unsurprisingly did little to help. The only thing that managed to bring Gertrude back from the brink was becoming pregnant again.

This troubling pattern would actually continue for seven more years. Gertrude would become pregnant, miscarry, and sink into despair. Only two of her pregnancies made it to full term; Shirley, the fifth child, and James, the sixth.

But John was still growing weary of his wife's incredible highs and intense lows. In 1963, he again filed for divorce, marking the beginning of what might be considered Gertrude's ultimate downward spiral in life.

The once-doting mother became almost as bitter towards her children as she was towards every other part of her life. By 1964, she was reportedly hitting them. In late October, John objected to her hitting Paula, to which Gertrude replied, "I will hit her any time or way or place I please!"

It was the first sign of something much darker to come.

IV

The Angry Young Lover

GERTRUDE'S NEXT PARTNER WAS DENNIS LEE Wright, an army man reportedly around nineteen to twenty-three years old when he met the thirty-six-year-old mother. The relationship was largely based on sex. It turned out Gertrude had a fondness for younger, less-experienced men, and Wright was more than content to be with a woman who was willing to put out, even if she did come with baggage in the form of six little ones.

Eventually, however, Gertrude wanted more from him. Seeing as they were already cohabiting and doing what she had been taught should only occur between a husband and a wife, she asked about getting married. Much to her disappointment, Wright was not interested—and he also did not want to have any children with her. In fact, the younger man was still married to another woman when he shacked up with the mother of six.

Much like Gertrude's prior two partners, Wright had a drinking problem. Along with sex, Gertrude used Wright's vice to her advantage, manipulating him into financially supporting her and her children. Such was her grasp on him that he did so without complaint, saying nothing even when she failed to keep up her end of the relationship.

Sex had, for so long, been a source of terror and shame, but now, for the first time in her life, it let her be in control—and she was not willing to give that up. When she sensed that Wright was planning on leaving her, she turned up the charm, becoming the ideal housewife until things were going her way again.

Despite her efforts, her reign over him would be short-lived. One evening, after having slept together, Gertrude tried to talk about marriage again, and this time she had another angle: she was likely pregnant with her seventh child. The spell she had cast over her young lover finally broke, and he became enraged.

He punched her, first in the face, then her abdomen. He was determined not to allow her to have his child because then he would never be free of her. Thoughts of his house, so dirty now with all her children running around and the constant noise flooded his mind. He had to get rid of her before it became a problem, his problem, for the rest of his life.

Just as he had hoped, Gertrude miscarried the next day.

This had not been the only instance of violence against her in this doomed relationship. Gertrude had already been used as Wright's ashtray; her arms and neck had numerous small, circular burns. Still, that treatment she believed she could withstand. It was what he did to the fetus that nearly broke her again.

The relationship existed in a strange sort of limbo from then on. Neither partner was happy, but they quietly kept up appearances. Wright would go to work, Gertrude would keep a somewhat clean home, and they would pretend that everything was fine. It would turn out that both were planning their next move, and unfortunately for Wright, Gertrude was one step ahead of him.

Once again, she became pregnant, but this time she was careful to keep it a secret until Wright could figure it out on his own, and by then, there was nothing he could do about it. Instead of the expected fury, Wright's reaction was far more subdued this time, almost apathetic. She mistook this apathy for acceptance and hoped that Wright would finally allow them to build a life together. She would even name the baby boy, her seventh and final child, after him.

Whatever hope she had clung onto was dashed the day she brought Dennis Wright Jr. home from the hospital. The elder Wright was nowhere to be found; he had picked up and abandoned her while she was having the baby. His calm reaction had been acceptance after all—not of parenthood, but of his plan to flee from his own home.

To make things even worse, her daughter Paula had done something especially shameful. She had abandoned her too, running off with some married man all the way to Kentucky.

If Gertrude's depressive episodes had been bad before, the one she experienced after these two events could only be described as her having finally hit rock bottom. She stopped eating regularly and quickly dropped to just one hundred pounds, which at her height of five foot six, was dangerously low. Her eyes had become sunken, and her skin pale. To her remaining children, it looked as if their mother was wasting away right before their eyes.

V
Two Wayward Girls

NOT FAR FROM GERTRUDE'S UNHAPPY HOME on 3850 New York Street, a different family was having problems of their own.

Lester and Betty Likens, parents to five children, loved each other, though they were prone to fighting. They had gotten married in 1944, and in their time together, they had moved around the country about nineteen times. Most of those moves were due to Lester's seeming inability to hold down a job for a long period. He had recently found work operating food stands at carnivals, though that only meant more traveling.

Betty had decided to separate from her husband for an undisclosed reason early in the summer of 1965. One day, she abruptly notified two of her daughters, sixteen-year-old Sylvia and fifteen-year-old Jenny Fay about her decision to move out of their apartment. Their mother appeared to have no particular place in mind as the three of them boarded a bus, but the girls were used to this kind of behavior from their parents, and they sat quietly beside her as the bus took them to the other side of town.

They stopped at a store where their mother looked around but did not purchase anything. When Sylvia and Jenny walked out of the building, an employee came after them, grabbing hold of their mother before she could get away. Betty had been caught shoplifting, and the police had been called. She handed her daughters around two dollars before she was taken to jail.

So Sylvia and Jenny were on their own. They walked around town, bought ice cream sodas with the money they were given, only to regret their purchase after they grew hungry. They called the women's prison to ask for their mother, but she was not there. After a while, they met up with a friend, Darlene McGuire, and the three of them went for a walk. Jenny hobbled just behind, as she wore a leg brace and walked with a noticeable limp after polio left one limb weaker than the other.

Sylvia, being older, was naturally protective of her disabled sister. They were together more often than not, and Sylvia took measures to make sure Jenny was included in whatever fun they sought out. Jenny would later recall going to roller skating rinks with Sylvia, the older girl holding her hands so that Jenny could skate on her good leg.

As hard as life could be, the two tried to make the best of it and were determined to see their current problems through as well. They spent the 4th of July alone in their mother's apartment, listening to the fireworks outside.

They spent some time at Darlene's house the next day but decided to go their separate ways for the day, Sylvia and their friend hopping in a car with another girl and Jenny heading back to the apartment to watch television with their landlady. Before long, however, Sylvia and Darlene were back, and they had brought with them another girl, Paula Baniszewski.

The Likens girls had not known the Baniszewski family before this, and Darlene had introduced them. Paula, it seemed, was nice enough, though Jenny was mildly off-put when the seventeen-year-old admitted she was two months pregnant. It would be the only time she would ever acknowledge the scandalous pregnancy, the result of a doomed affair with an older married man. Paula had run off with him to Hazard, Kentucky, and had to come home to her mother when he ended up rejecting the chubby teenager.

If the girls noticed anything odd about the Baniszewskis, they made no mention of it that first day. In fact, when they first met Gertrude, they likely felt sorry for her. Many people in the neighborhood pitied the emaciated, sickly-looking woman with her rambunctious brood of seven. Things had gone downhill for her after her common-law husband and daughter left her. She had since won a paternity suit that meant more child support, and Paula had come home but was not yet coping any better.

The house was dirty, and money was tight, but Gertrude was cordial enough with the Likens girls. She was used to being around teenagers, including those who weren't her own. Ever since her mental health worsened, Paula had taken over many of the household duties, giving her the authority to do as she pleased. She invited friends over, and soon, the house became a hotspot for teenagers. If Gertrude minded, she didn't have the strength to object. It was likely how Darlene had come to know them.

The four of them spent the afternoon drinking soda and listening to records, and for an afternoon, they were the image of mid-century normalcy—minus the ailing Gertrude in the next room. When evening came, Paula asked if they could stay for dinner. Gertrude said yes, Jenny could stay but notably did not invite Sylvia. She only gave in when Jenny said she could not stay if Sylvia was not with her.

The girls ended up spending the night instead. It was Shirley Baniszewski's tenth birthday, and by midnight, everyone was still awake to celebrate. The festivities were interrupted when two men knocked on the front door.

"It's my daddy and brother, Danny," Jenny explained before Lester asked them to come out.

"Where's Mommy?" he asked. He was tired and anxious, he had gone to Betty's apartment and found it empty. If he hadn't run into Darlene, he would have had a much harder time locating his daughters.

They explained that their mother had been arrested.

Lester, it turned out, had arrived with interesting news. He was going back on the road with the carnival company to manage the food stands, but he wanted to make up with his wife first. Not only that, but he also wanted to take her with him.

Gertrude invited the two men in, but Lester needed to find Betty. However, before going to look for her at the prison, Lester and Danny went to buy White Castle burgers, bringing enough to share with Gertrude and her brood. He later found Betty had already been released but did not go back to her apartment.

Frustrated and exhausted, he returned to the Baniszewski home, and Lester explained the situation. He and his wife were going away, and they needed someone to watch their children while they were gone. Along with Danny, the nineteen-year-old twin to the already married and distant Diana, Jenny also had a twin, Benny. Sylvia was the odd one out, a single girl between two sets of twins. He was bringing his children to stay with his mother in his hometown of Lebanon, Indiana. This interested Gertrude, who quickly saw a money-making opportunity. Seeing how his girls were already friends with her daughter, why not let them stay at her house? She would charge twenty dollars a week, around a hundred and fifty in today's currency. It was certainly a tempting offer, especially since Lester's mother would have likely struggled with four unruly teenagers. The girls themselves seemed to be pleased with the arrangement.

Lester and Danny stayed over as well, giving Lester a chance to sleep on the offer. He wanted to ask Betty's opinion first, and in the morning, he found her at her parent's house. They reconciled, as they had many times before. After filling her in on his work plans and the Baniszewskis, she also agreed to let her daughters board with Gertrude.

So, the plan was set. Lester gave Gertrude a twenty in advance. He hoped the hard-working mother would straighten his sometimes mischievous daughters out and even advised her to use a "firm hand" when disciplining them.

The unsuspecting father could have never known the weight his words would come to carry.

VI

The Bad Times Begin

THE FIRST WEEK WENT BY WITHOUT A HITCH. If Gertrude had already come to dislike Sylvia, she managed to keep it to herself. The hot summer days stretched by quietly. Sylvia and Jenny divided their time between hanging out with Paula, listening to records and talking about boys, and helping Gertrude with the housework, which Sylvia was said to have done happily.

But the warm facade Gertrude had put on when she met Lester Likens was starting to slip. Neither he, Betty, nor Danny had seen any part of the house beyond the living room, and neither had any idea how badly the family had been doing. There was no stove, so the family's scant meals of toast or soup were cooked on a single hot plate. The Baniszewskis had three spoons, but soon they only had one that they were forced to take turns sharing between them all.

Arguments often broke out when one sibling accused the other of taking more than their fair share of food. Their dwelling was cramped, with more children than there were beds.

Poverty had long been a part of Gertrude's life and it was starting to show. She worked sixteen hour days and had a house full of children, including several neighbors. She was stressed out and nervous at every moment of her life. Chronic illnesses like bronchitis and asthma had weakened her already frail body, and the medications she was prescribed, stimulants and sedatives alike, only exacerbated her mental instability. She was welcoming at times and hostile at others, shrieking at the children to get out and give her some peace. So Paula and Sylvia went to the park, Jenny limping behind them.

One might have expected Gertrude to have been thankful for the help Sylvia gave, but she was rapidly reaching her breaking point. That point seemingly came when Lester's money arrived late. She dragged the Likens girls upstairs and slapped Jenny across the face. "I took care of you two bitches for a week for nothing!"

The money order arrived the following morning.

On July 17th, the Likens girls met two more members of the Baniszewski clan. Fifteen-year-old Stephanie and twelve-year-old Johnny had come home after spending time at their father's house. Though Stephanie was surprised to see that strangers had moved in while she was away, she nevertheless quickly grew friendly with Sylvia.

The Likens parents came to visit not long after. The Likens girls made no mention of their mistreatment. Perhaps, given the culture of the 1960s, when physical discipline against children was still widely accepted, they thought little of it. Certainly, they didn't anticipate the levels of depravity the entire Baniszewski clan would soon sink to. Lester gave Gertrude another twenty dollars, and then he and Betty were on their way. Before he left, however, he told his daughters that they could spend their time at the park picking up bottles to recycle. The money they made could help the family out.

Unfortunately, Gertrude did not take this well. She thought the Likens girls were making her children loiter around, and she decided they needed to be punished for making them look bad. This time, however, she did not bother with slapping them. Gertrude found a variety of items around the house that she used to dole out discipline, including a black leather police belt that John Sr. had left for exactly that purpose. More commonly, she used a quarter-inch-thick wooden fraternity paddle on their backsides. On Sylvia, she used it on the back of her head.

When Gertrude felt too weak, she handed the paddle to Paula, who had no problem hitting the girls, sometimes much harder than her mother did.

Still, things were not yet nearly as grim as they would get. That first month, the Likens girls did have some fun every now and then. Paula would sometimes still play nice with them, and the mean streak she and her mother had was seemingly absent in Stephanie. They would go on frequent outings to the local park, but it was the church that provided them with a much-needed reprieve from the chaos.

Gertrude, who had taken to calling herself Mrs Wright and insisting that her husband was just away in the army, had a powerful need to keep up appearances. She made sure to send her children to the Memorial Baptist Church every Sunday, though she rarely attended herself. After church services ended, the girls would have an opportunity to socialize and sometimes get a meal without Gertrude's angry eyes on them.

On August 22nd, the Likens and Baniszewski girls confessed their faith before the entire congregation. This pleased the Reverend Julian, but others weren't as convinced about Paula. One Sunday, she arrived at church with a cast on her wrist and reportedly bragged to a woman that she had broken it after punching Sylvia in the jaw. "I tried to kill her," she admitted with a grin.

Paula's reasoning was that Sylvia had called her mother a nasty name. There was no proof of this, but the truth mattered little in Gertrude's household. It soon became a more and more frequent occurrence for them to completely make up reasons to justify abusing Sylvia to each other, ranging from probable to bizarre. Gertrude accused her of having stolen ten dollars out of her purse, so she got paddled. Paula accused her of having eaten more than her fair share at a church potluck, so she got clubbed over a dozen times on her back. Marie saw her eat a sandwich that Dianna had brought her, so she got slapped. Gertrude believed that she smelled mustard on Sylvia's breath, meaning that Danny had bought her a burger that she did not share, so she yanked her by the hair until she collapsed onto the floor.

Gluttony, as fabricated as it was, was a particularly perverse sin in a house where everyone often had no choice but to go hungry. Gertrude raged about how much Sylvia supposedly ate and called her a pig. In reality, Sylvia was eating as little as the rest of them, spending her days struck by hunger pains. Whatever Gertrude's strange thought process was, she never let up her disgust, and soon found a new way to punish the girl.

One day, Gertrude and Paula, joined by a neighbor boy named Randy Lepper, sat Sylvia down at the kitchen table and decided to teach her a lesson. They took turns loading a hot dog with various toppings and spices, passing it around to each other until mustard was spilling onto the floor. Then they tried to get Sylvia to eat it.

Sylvia refused, but Gertrude wasn't having it.

The woman forced the hot dog into Sylvia's mouth, smearing the condiments all over her face. Sylvia coughed and gagged and tried to get away, but she was held down as Gertrude jammed it into her mouth, hitting the back of her throat. "Eat it, you bitch!" Gertrude shrieked as she tried to pry Sylvia's jaw open.

The frightened teenager cried and tried to do as she was ordered, but the sludge of condiments was overpowering. Gertrude's fingers were deep inside her mouth now, still shoving pieces of meat and bun down her throat. Sylvia couldn't help it; she vomited all over the kitchen floor.

Sylvia, exhausted and sick, hoped the ordeal was done with. However, Gertrude insisted she was not done. If she really wanted to be finished, then she had to have eaten every last bit of the hot dog—including the bits she had regurgitated onto the floor.

Once she had sunken down to her hands and knees onto the unkempt kitchen floor, Gertrude grabbed a fistful of her long hair and yanked her over to the steaming puddle. Sylvia feebly crawled forward and lapped up her own vomit while her three tormentors laughed around her.

VII

A Jealous Rage

THOUGH JENNY WAS BY NO MEANS SAFE FROM Gertrude and Paula's abuse, they had, by now, turned their cruel attention almost entirely on her sister. The exact reason they both decided to turn Sylvia into their scapegoat is unclear. Notable, however, is the fact that Gertrude was reliving the same dynamic that had made her own childhood a living hell. This time, she was in her mother's place, though even Mollie Van Fossan had never sunk to such depravity.

Sylvia, nicknamed Cookie by her friends, was a pretty and decently popular teenager. Boys liked her. For all her family's dysfunction, her parents loved her, as they did all of their children.

Her future, at least until she stepped foot in the Baniszewski home, looked bright. Perhaps, in Sylvia, Gertrude saw a glimpse of the kind of life she might have had if she had just been a tiny bit luckier, a life where people were kind and home was a happy place. To see the kind of existence that had been denied to her must have tortured Gertrude.

Paula, on the other hand, was a much stranger case. She and Gertrude were close, sometimes in an almost maniacal way. She became her mother's ready and willing henchwoman. Overweight and saddled with too much responsibility, she likely shared her mother's hateful jealousy of their guest. It didn't help that she had a secret that would doubtlessly ruin her reputation, one that she and Gertrude continued to deny even as the summer months dragged on. It became increasingly obvious to anyone who saw her. That this slim, pretty girl who was taking up space—her space—in the house knew her secret was intolerable.

Jenny, with her timid nature and visible disability, was less detestable in her misfortune.

In her book *The Basement: Meditations on a Human Sacrifice*, feminist writer Kate Millett argues that the crimes committed against Sylvia were rooted, in many ways, in sex, both in the act and the biological sense. Indeed, Sylvia's sexuality and supposed promiscuity became a point of obsession for Gertrude, who had developed a sense of resentment for the female sex during her tormented youth.

"Women are unclean creatures," she would say. "God doesn't love them the way he loves men."

We can see some proof of Millett's assertion during an afternoon they all shared together. In the time following the hot dog incident, Gertrude and Paula seemed calmer, less antagonistic. The topic of boys and dating came up. It was a fun conversation at first, but it also felt so normal. Sylvia and Jenny, trapped in a house of hatred, were suddenly typical teenagers again. Stephanie filled them in on her new boyfriend, Coy Hubbard, a tall, athletic fifteen-year-old. Paula, still in denial about her pregnancy, kept tight about the details of her love life, though she did admit to some experience. Jenny mentioned having kissed a boy once.

Sylvia was reminded of happier times spent on the West Coast. She would have liked to have stayed in Long Beach, California. There was a boy she met there she had liked, but her parents, homesick for their home state, brought them all back to Indiana.

This piqued Gertrude's curiosity. "Have you ever done anything with a boy, Sylvia?"

Sure, she had done a lot of things with them; she had hung out with boys, gone skating with them, and sometimes went to parties with them. Sylvia must have not understood the trap Gertrude was leading her into. After some more pressing, Sylvia mentioned a party she held back in Long Beach while her parents had been away. She and her boyfriend had kissed often and on that night, she even allowed him to touch her body.

Suddenly the mood was dead. Everyone fell silent.

Gertrude looked at her. She was frowning. "Why did you do that, Sylvia?"

"I don't know," Sylvia replied.

Really there was nothing the unsuspecting teenager could have said that would have shaken off Gertrude's disapproval. The woman had already made up her mind about hating her. Innocent words would be made twisted to justify the rage that was constantly simmering beneath the surface.

But sex was something in a league of its own. Gertrude despised sex like she despised Sylvia. She knew its power, knew how it could ruin a person. If having sex made you bad, then that meant that Sylvia was bad, and if Sylvia was bad, then it no longer mattered how hard Gertrude slapped her or how ugly the names she called her were. In Gertrude's eyes, Sylvia deserved it all and worse.

The Baniszewskis would not allow Sylvia to forget what she admitted to them. It started off light with some teasing. "You're getting big in the stomach," Gertrude told her some days later. "You look like you're going to have a baby."

Sylvia tried to laugh it off. "Yeah, I guess I am. I'm just gonna have to go on a diet."

They were serious, deadly serious. Gertrude was disgusted. She told Sylvia that she was filthy, that she had allowed herself to be ruined by sex and a boy's touch. As Sylvia tried to get away, Gertrude kicked and stomped on her groin, screaming all the while that she was a whore.

When aching Sylvia tried to sit, Paula got involved. "You ain't fit to sit in a chair," she said as she knocked Sylvia to the floor.

The accusation would have a profound effect on Sylvia's psyche. Somehow, even as she grew skinnier and skinnier, Sylvia became convinced she was pregnant.

VIII
Back to School

IN LATE AUGUST, LESTER AND BETTY PAID THEIR daughters another visit. Everything was going fine, or so they were told. Sylvia and Jenny reported no mistreatment. If they had bruises, their parents did not see them. The only hint they ever gave that something was amiss was telling them that they were hungry, so they all went out for a burger at the local drive-in, and that was the end of that.

Those of us looking back on this story through the lens of court transcripts and newspaper archives probably wondered how exactly Gertrude managed to pull it off for so long. How did she get away with the horrible things she was doing to the Likens girls when their parents were right in her house? They paid multiple visits to 3850 New York Street throughout that summer. Surely a pair of loving parents would have noticed that something was amiss—and the girls themselves, would speak up when they had the chance.

Unfortunately, the girls did not speak up for the same reason many other abused children did not say something: they were simply too afraid. What if nobody believed them? What if Gertrude found out that they had told on her? What would she do to them then? Jenny would explain as such on the witness stand months later.

The sad truth was that things were not yet as bad as they would get.

In early September, Gertrude would continue to keep up appearances by sending the Likens girls to school. Sylvia, who had dropped out of high school around her sixteenth birthday that January, was actually looking forward to Arsenal Tech. It guaranteed a few hours a day away from Gertrude's wrath, as well as at least one hot meal that she could eat with some dignity. She took a job in the cafeteria in hopes of earning a little extra money.

For all the trouble she was having with her mother and sister, Sylvia could still count Stephanie as her friend. The time they spent together, joking around or singing their favorite songs to each other, made the misery that had become Sylvia's life just a little more bearable. It was through Stephanie that Sylvia met and befriended Coy Hubbard. The latter friendship would soon prove to be short-lived.

In Sylvia's time at school, we see what was perhaps the one known instance of her fighting back against the abuse she endured. She told a male classmate that the Baniszewski girls were prostitutes, and for the right price, they would go to bed with him. The boy would bluntly ask Stephanie how much she charged the next time he ran into her.

"What are you talking about?" she asked, confused.

"How much do you want to go to bed with me?"

Stephanie became angry. "Who told you I do that?"

"A friend of yours," he admitted. "Her name is Sylvia."

"Some friend," Stephanie scoffed. When she returned home that day, she looked for Sylvia and punched her in the jaw. Sylvia began to cry, admitted what she had done and apologized to her friend. Stephanie began to cry too; she did not enjoy hurting Sylvia.

Had Sylvia been more careful, the single punch she received from Stephanie would have been the only consequence she'd face for her mean-spirited mistake. However, the rumors had spread quicker than she had ever anticipated. Paula knew, and so did Johnny, but it was Coy Hubbard who decided to take matters into his own hands.

Coy was tall for his age and strong too. He was learning judo and set out to get some practice by beating the girl who had insulted his girlfriend's honor. When he found Sylvia, he grabbed her head, banging it back against the wall. When she stood, dazed from the blow, he grabbed hold of her again and flipped her hard onto her back to the floor.

Later, after Johnny had told Gertrude about the rumors, she gave the girl a paddling.

School started to look far less appealing after that.

Naturally, Gertrude did her part in making school a living hell for Sylvia. When Sylvia, who had been assigned a gym class that term, asked Gertrude for some money to purchase the appropriate clothing, Gertrude refused. Lester may have given the girls some cash for school expenses that month, but that money belonged to Gertrude now. All the money in the house went to Gertrude's medication and cigarettes, then food. It certainly was not going to go to Sylvia after the nasty things she had said about her daughters.

Sylvia managed to get around this problem when she found some gym clothes on the ground, but that angered Gertrude. She arrived back at the house with her find only to be welcomed with a slap to the face and accusations of being a thief. Then she had to endure being beaten with John Sr.'s leather police belt.

Whenever Gertrude got angry, she became prone to going on tirades. She had just finished whipping Sylvia black and blue when she sat the girl down and began to lecture her about her promiscuity. Stephanie tried to intervene when her mother repeatedly kicked Sylvia in the groin.

Stephanie cried, and Gertrude called Coy to tell him that Sylvia had hurt his girlfriend again. The love-struck teenager showed up at the Baniszewski house immediately, and Gertrude got him to help her when she lit a match to Sylvia's fingers.

Life for Sylvia had become a never-ending torrent of punishment. If she wasn't being beaten, she was being insulted. Now she knew what would happen to her if she tried to lash out in any way, no matter how minuscule.

"I hate you! You're ruining my life!" Gertrude yelled, too tired from beating her to continue.

In September, the entire household had started growing worried about Stephanie.

Stephanie Baniszewski had always been the brains in the family. Her younger siblings called her "Einstein" or "Einey" for short because the worst grades she ever got were Bs. Gertrude had never finished high school. Paula, while still enrolled in evening classes, was less concerned with her education now that she was suffering from a condition that grew more noticeable every passing day. Stephanie, on the other hand, had big dreams of becoming a lawyer someday and tried to miss as little school as possible.

It was to her great dismay that she now had to stay home because she was experiencing random fainting spells throughout the day. They were growing more frequent, and doctors were having trouble finding the cause of them. Fearing the worst, the Baniszewskis next turned to God.

The preacher at Memorial Baptist Church was Reverend Roy Julian. He was young and said to have been a handsome man which made it easier for his sermons to hold the attention of bored teenage girls, but he was well-liked for other reasons. Always concerned about the souls of his congregation, he could always be counted on to visit whenever he was called. Sometime that month, Gertrude asked him to come to pray with her for her daughter's health.

The truth was that Reverend Julian was already worried about the Baniszewskis. Though Gertrude sent her entire brood of hungry children to service on Sundays, he had never actually seen the woman herself among them. Still, he knew she was a busy, hard-working woman, and he wanted to offer some guidance—especially since he had heard some troubling rumors about her daughters.

Gertrude made sure to get as much sympathy as she could out of him as soon as he stepped through her front door. "I don't feel so good," she said as she led him to the couch. "Sometimes, I can hardly catch my breath. I've been taking this new medicine the doctor gave for my bronchitis, but it affects me just as bad. It dopes me up—I have to spend half the day in bed." She gave him a sad look. "My husband don't pay the support like he should. I'm trying to keep the family going with the ironing, but the customers are getting impatient with me."

He nodded, listening intently. Together, they prayed in silence for a while before he asked her about her children. She shook her head and sighed. "Oh, they're just running wild. The children—mostly Sylvia—are causing me quite a few problems. They're giving me quite a bad case of the nerves. I have to take medicine for that too. The doctor gave me some phenobarbital," she explained. "I had to start correcting the children. I tried to spank Sylvia once, but I couldn't because of my asthma. Paula had to help me."

The Reverend asked her to tell him more about Sylvia, and Gertrude jumped at the chance to air out her grievances.

"She's been skipping school and making advances on older men for money. I had to start locking her up in her room upstairs because she would slip out at night."

"May I speak with Sylvia?"

Gertrude hesitated. She knew she could not give Sylvia a single chance to contradict her narrative. To her relief, Jenny had passed by the next room at that moment. "Well, here's her sister. You can ask her."

"What about your sister, child?" he asked as Jenny hobbled over.

Jenny's face went pale. She swallowed down her nervousness and said, "She tells lies, and at night, after all of us go to bed, she goes downstairs and raids the icebox."

"She took the baby's milk once," Gertrude added.

The Reverend could not help but feel disappointed by what he had heard that day. Sylvia, along with Stephanie, had been among the most engaged and enthusiastic of all the church's Sunday school students. It was a shame that she had such a change of heart. He prayed for her soul again one last time before he left the house, hoping to save her from eternal damnation. According to her caretaker, it sure sounded like that's where the girl was headed.

IX
The Ringleader

IT WAS NOT ENOUGH THAT SHE HATED SYLVIA, Gertrude saw to it that others did as well. So far, she had managed to turn most of her children against the girl, and now for the first time, Gertrude saw something positive come out of Paula, having turned her home into a flophouse for noisy teenagers. All the nice neighborhood kids would soon become part of Gertrude's wicked game.

Sylvia's attendance at school had gone from perfect to spotty, and by now she had all but dropped out again. With all those bruises and her sickly look from constant hunger, Gertrude was no longer keen on keeping Sylvia out of the house. Without her at school, friends came by looking for Sylvia. One of those friends was Anna Siscoe, an innocent and somewhat naive thirteen-year-old Sylvia had grown close with before her disappearance.

In this nice girl that Gertrude found yet another opportunity to brutalize Sylvia. When Anna showed up at her doorstep, Gertrude swooped in before Sylvia could even greet her. "Sylvia said your mother goes out with all sorts of men for five dollars," Gertrude whispered. It got her the reaction she wanted. Anna was in disbelief.

When Sylvia appeared, Anna slapped her, then kicked her. Somehow, she also managed to scratch up Sylvia's entire back.

Some of the other kids present at the house at that time tried to pull the girls off each other, but Gertrude would not allow anyone to intervene. "Let them fight their own fight," she told them.

Sylvia would never again make the mistake of trying to defend herself. Soon she was on the ground, writhing in pain. Anna kicked her again, this time square in the abdomen. Sylvia moaned in pain and cried out for the baby she was convinced she was carrying.

It was only when Anna managed to calm down that she realized the truth. Even so, it would not be the only time that Anna would be convinced to attack her supposed friend.

Beatings became a sort of game. Someone would get angry with Sylvia over something Gertrude made up, and then they would assault her. The others, including Stephanie, would then join in. "Everybody's having fun with Sylvia," said Richard Hobbs. The preteen's idea of fun included punching, flipping, and ultimately, branding Sylvia.

So why did so many teenagers who, by all appearances, had no great interest in violence end up ganging up against one girl? Perhaps Johnny's own words can shed some light on the barbarism that happened at 3850 New York Street.

Everybody's having fun with Sylvia. Everybody. If you were not part of everybody, then you were nobody. Who would want to stand out in a house like this? Even Jenny was convinced by Gertrude to slap her own sister, or else the game would have turned on her. The poor girl reportedly used her non-dominant hand to minimize the pain.

The days were a frenzy. Almost overnight, Sylvia had gone from having two or three tormentors to an entire gang of them.

Sometimes up to ten of the neighborhood children, would toy with her, kick her around, punch her in the face, put out cigarettes on her skin.

Anger was not the only thing that motivated them. The boys, in particular appeared, to have attacked Sylvia less due to perceived slights but simply because they could. No one was getting in trouble for hurting Sylvia; in fact, the only adult in the house condoned it, so why not let loose? So Sylvia became a punching bag for their frustrations and dark desires.

They laughed. Always, they laughed. Sylvia would crawl away but the sounds of it always surrounded her like a chorus to her never-ending nightmare.

Still, not all the Baniszewski kids were having fun. The nonstop violence was getting to Stephanie, making her anxious. She was the closest thing that Sylvia had to a friend besides Jenny and she didn't like seeing her get hurt. There were times where she tried to step in either by snatching weapons out of Paula's hands or insisting to her mother, always in vain, that Sylvia was innocent of whatever latest indiscretion she had been accused of. Unfortunately, Stephanie soon found herself having more stress than she could handle over the whole thing and her fainting spells increased.

"Fighting! Fighting! That's all we ever do around here!" she wailed out of the blue one evening. "I just wish we'd quit!"

Gertrude made sure to point out her daughter's distress to Coy Hubbard. Coy, never one to allow his girlfriend to be disrespected, quickly sought out Sylvia to make her pay.

It wouldn't be long before Gertrude would manage to turn Stephanie against Sylvia too.

When Sylvia could no longer withstand her constant hunger, she snuck out of the house at night in search of food. By then, the pain had become unbearable, leaving her constantly dazed and weak. A lack of proper nutrition meant that the countless wounds that covered her body would not heal. She had become a walking collection of bruises, burns, and open sores.

Sylvia dug through trash cans in her desperate state, picking out scraps of food and collecting whatever glass bottles she could find. The bottles proved to be the better of her two choices because she could trade them in to buy herself an actual meal. When she had at last eaten, she tried to sneak back into the house.

Her night's luck, as it turned out, ended when she stepped through the door.

Gertrude had been waiting for her along with some of the boys. Jenny was there, too, and she looked afraid, as though she already had some idea what this gang had in store for her sister.

The woman had something familiar in her hand. A glass soda bottle.

Gertrude barked at her to get naked, accusing her of being a prostitute as the trembling girl stripped out of her clothes. The boys got closer, watching intently as Sylvia fumbled with her bra and panties.

Then Gertrude handed her the bottle. "Give them a show, whore."

Sylvia could barely wrap her mind around what she was being ordered to do. She stared at the bottle in her hand and held back a cry. Around her, the boys with their hungry eyes were growing impatient. Gertrude had promised them a show, and if they didn't get it, they would likely make her do something worse.

But what could be more humiliating than this? It was even worse with Jenny here because Sylvia knew this was also a punishment for her—and it was all her fault. If she hadn't snuck out, poor Jenny wouldn't have gotten in trouble for allowing it.

"Go on," said Gertrude. "You know you want to. Why don't you show your sister the kind of girl you really are?"

Sylvia steeled her nerves and placed the bottle upright on the floor. There was no other option. She shut her eyes and squat down, her tired legs were spread wide open, and everyone could see her vagina. With one hand, she reached for the bottle and inserted the glass neck inside her body.

It was painful. Despite what Gertrude had told everyone, Sylvia had never done anything like this before. She had never even slept with the only boyfriend she ever had. Now here she was, wincing as she tried to shove the bottle further in while boys hooted and hollered at the sight of it.

She tried to move the thing but the cold glass would hardly give. What if it broke, she wondered. Would they make her keep going?

The show was going on too slowly for Gertrude. When her demands that Sylvia do something a little more amusing with herself were met only with more cries, the woman took it upon herself to smack the bottom of the bottle with her palm until it could go in no further.

Perhaps it was Sylvia's agonized shrieks that got Stephanie's attention. Her friend hurried into the room and came face to face with the horrifying scene. Stephanie gasped in disbelief.

Rather than feel sorry for Sylvia, Stephanie was infuriated with her. How could she allow herself to be debased like this—and in front of Stephanie's own little brother? Had her mother been right about Sylvia all along?

Stephanie shoved her way past weeping Jenny and leering boys and smacked Sylvia hard across the face. "Go on up to your room, Sylvia!" she shouted as tried to get her to stand.

There was a problem, of course. There was no way she could stand like this, much less climb the stairs. The bottle was still stuck inside—and Sylvia couldn't get it out.

Gertrude, annoyed at the show having ended so abruptly, yanked the bottle out herself. There was a noticeable amount of blood pooled at the bottom.

Things were tense between Sylvia and Stephanie after that.

It had not taken much for Gertrude to convince them all to do her dirty work. After all, she had managed to build a repertoire with them already thanks to Paula; Gertrude was, in the eyes of restless teenagers, the "cool" adult, their friend's mom who let them come over whenever they pleased and smoke under her roof. She was less of a mom and just another one of their friends. What more, she was their confidant. Whenever Sylvia had supposedly insulted them, Gertrude would make sure to fill them in right away.

It was important for Gertrude to keep the game going. These days, her asthma and bronchitis were leaving her too weak to pummel the girl herself, so she was glad she had so many kids willing to step in.

Her own young daughters, Shirley and Marie, were just as vicious as the rest. When twelve-year-old Judy Duke confronted Sylvia for having called her a bitch, Shirley jumped in and tore the buttons off Sylvia's blouse, leaving her exposed in front of a group of boys. Sylvia fell to the floor and Anna began to stomp on her abdomen. When Sylvia began to cry again for the baby that wasn't there, Judy, so full of rage just a moment ago, hurried home feeling sick.

It was around this time that Paula did something rather peculiar. After so many evenings spent pelting Sylvia with glass soda bottles and dinner plates, it seemed the pregnant teenager suddenly had a change of heart. "Get away and stay away," she instructed, holding the back door open. "Get out for your own safety."

But Sylvia went nowhere. She stayed put, despite the warnings from her own tormentor. Why didn't she run, so many would later ask. Surely, she must have at least considered it at some point, so why did she stay? The Likens girls had their grandmother in Lebanon and another family member in the same city. Their sister Dianna was around somewhere, and they were unsure where exactly she lived now, but there had to be some way to contact her. There were workers at the park they frequented that they could have asked for help. The staff at Arsenal Tech could have done something for them, so why did Sylvia all but give up?

In reality, the teenager now spent every moment of her life in abject terror. She was scared of leaving Jenny behind or getting caught and suffering worse punishment than ever before. Lack of food and sleep, combined with the constant beatings, left her too weak to run. In her eyes, there was really nowhere she could go.

She was practically an orphan now, hopelessly trapped with a cruel guardian.

Gertrude had effectively broken her spirit.

X
A Thread of Hope

IF THERE WAS ANY HOPE TO STILL BE HAD IN Gertrude's house of torture, it came on October 5th. Lester and Betty went to visit the girls again, and they were happy to announce that it would be their last. Over another drive-in meal—as the girls, just like every other time they had seen each other, confessed to them that they were quite hungry—Lester shared some more exciting news. With summer over, the carnival season was coming to an end. He and his wife were due back home in three weeks.

Their parents then returned them to that dragon's den. They watched their father hand Gertrude another twenty dollars for the week. Betty handed them each school clothes they had purchased along with some extra money for shoes.

Three weeks. That was less than a month. Three weeks was all they had to endure before they could leave behind this horrible place. They had been with Gertrude for three months now, what was a few more weeks?

Sylvia knew she had to be strong for Jenny—and for herself. Her tormentors had beaten her down and degraded her, but she still wanted to live. The end of her nightmare was finally in sight.

Something indeed would take place in three weeks, but it would be something that nobody, not even Gertrude and her circus of teenagers, ever expected.

Sylvia went back to Arsenal Tech the following day with a little more reason to keep pushing through. Allowing her to leave the house may have been a mistake on Gertrude's part. Sylvia's spotty attendance the previous month meant that school administrators had already notified her about their concerns several times. Gertrude had managed to get them off her back by portraying herself as a worried caretaker whose charge was simply uninterested in her education.

If they saw Sylvia again in the state that she was, alarm bells would go off. After all, some neighbors had already noticed strange behavior from the battered girl, like catching her eating from trash cans. Someone else on their street had heard somebody scream for hours one night, though luckily for Gertrude, that neighbor did not bother to call the police.

Sylvia would not return to school on the seventh, nor would she go back on any of the following days. From then on, Gertrude made sure to keep her in the house where nobody could see her.

Even though Sylvia was no longer allowed to go out and be seen, Gertrude had slightly less control over who could get in and see her. Very shortly after the visit from the Likens parents, the Baniszewskis found themselves with some new next-door neighbors.

The Vermillions were a nice middle-class family, though some might have not expected it given the neighborhood they had little choice but to move into. The truth was that New York Street, while not a slum, was hardly in a desirable area. If a new family moved in, it meant that they were having trouble with money more often than not. That was certainly the case for the

Likens and the Baniszewskis, who struggled each month to pay the fifty-five-dollar rent, but less so for the Vermillions.

Both Robert and Phyllis Vermillion held steady jobs. In particular, Mrs. Vermillion worked a full-time evening shift at the Radio Corporation of America. It meant that she needed a full-time babysitter for her two young children. She had heard from around that Mrs. Wright, as Gertrude was still calling herself, had quite a lot of experience watching children.

Mrs. Vermillion was a bit unsure if she could leave her children with a stranger as the weary woman already had to take care of nine children, but she went over in the morning just to introduce herself. What she would see in that house would stick with her for a long, long time.

Gertrude had been courteous enough to let her in, but Mrs. Vermillion could not shake the feeling that her neighbor was feeling tense, almost anxious at her presence. Indeed, the house, filthy and full of noise, was unwelcoming. By the time Gertrude offered her a cup of coffee, Mrs. Vermillion just wanted to get out of there.

Even so, Mrs. Vermillion found Mrs. Wright to be a little more likable than she initially let on. Perhaps it was because she was so easy to feel sorry for. Nine children, including four teenagers and one crying toddler, could not be easy to care for on her own. She had heard that Mrs. Wright needed to do all kinds of things to make ends meet, from doing other people's laundry to selling snacks along the motorway. Her husband, Mr. Dennis Wright, was in the army and currently stationed somewhere far, far away. The toll it was all taking on her was obvious; if you told her that the frail, sunken-eyed mother was not yet forty years old, Mrs. Vermillion may not have believed it.

While they sat and chatted, Mrs. Vermillion saw the teenagers in the dining room. Mrs. Wright's two daughters, the older of whom was obviously pregnant, were accompanied by another girl. The girl seated at the table was worryingly thin. She was hunched over, as though she was trying to make herself appear as small as possible, like she was trying to disappear.

When the girl lifted her face, Mrs. Vermillion was stunned to see her bruised face.

"Why, child," she could not help but ask. "How did you get that black eye?"

Something about her question made the girl nervous. She gave no reply. Instead, she just looked away. The question appeared to have made Mrs. Wright nervous too. She stood and stomped over to the dining room. "Get out of my sight! Get out of here! I don't want nothing to do with you, Sylvia!" demanded Mrs. Wright as the girl hurried away. "I hate you!"

Mrs. Wright looked back at her new neighbor. "That's Sylvia," she explained, her disgust evident.

Mrs. Vermillion watched Sylvia slink away into the kitchen. There the pregnant girl joined her. Mrs. Wright's eldest daughter turned the hot water faucet on the sink and filled up a cup. Out of nowhere, entirely unprovoked, she threw the steaming water into Sylvia's bruised face.

If that had not been barbaric enough, the pregnant girl then took some margarine out of the fridge and smeared the oily substance all over Sylvia. Mrs. Vermillion watched in silent horror. The way Sylvia cried out made her blood run cold.

Yet Mrs. Wright—and seemingly everyone else present in the house—had no reaction to this. Did the woman just let her children do as they pleased? Were they all angry with Sylvia? Whatever she had done in their eyes to deserve that treatment, it must have been something unspeakable.

Paula, as she learned the eldest was named, handed Mrs. Vermillion a mug of coffee. "I gave her the black eye," she said, sounding rather proud of herself.

She glanced back at Paula's mother, who did not look displeased at the confession, but her mood changed again when she saw Sylvia still lingering in the next room. "Go on up to your room, Sylvia! Go on! If you don't, I'm gonna kill you!"

It was like the woman's moods were controlled by a switch. Suddenly, she was calm again, looking at her neighbor with exhausted eyes. "Her parents are down south chasing some carnival. She's three months pregnant and hasn't had her period in three months! Can you believe that?"

Mrs. Wright tutted and shook her head with disapproval. "I just don't know what I'm gonna do with her."

Mrs. Vermillion was wise enough to find another babysitter for her own children, though she decided to remain friendly with the Baniszewskis. She probably figured that Mrs. Wright had just been stressed out from too much work and that Sylvia was a troublemaker because that was the story that Gertrude told everyone. In any case, the two women maintained an amicable not-quite-friendship that October, and before long Mrs. Vermillion would pay another visit.

She was shocked to see Sylvia in an even worse state this time. The girl was listless and silent, almost ghost-like. Every part of her body that Mrs. Vermillion could see was bruised, and that black eye of hers had either failed to heal or she had gotten another one since her last visit. Her lip was red and swollen, and from the looks of it, it had been bleeding too.

What in the world was going on in this house?

Paula must have caught her look of horror. "She's nothing but trouble. I had to beat her up again." As soon as she said this, she went off to get a thick leather belt.

This time, Sylvia did not need to be chased out of the room. She stood up automatically, as though she knew this was part of a routine already. The two girls left the room and a moment later, Mrs. Vermillion heard the unmistakable sound of leather against flesh.

She winced. There were no cries from Sylvia this time.

"Does Sylvia go to school?" Mrs. Vermillion asked.

Mrs. Wright made a sour face. "I had to make her quit school 'cause she was a thief. She stole somebody's gym clothes at school and then she stole from the neighbors too. All she does is cause us problems," she explained. She took a long drag from her cigarette and let out a sigh. It seemed like she was always smoking. "I don't know how I'm gonna repay all the people. Guess I'll just have to take some of the money she's been making."

It is unclear what Mrs. Vermillion believed, but she decided not to get involved. Some might say that she was just trying to mind her own business, that she did not want to cause further issues for poor, sickly Mrs. Wright. However, she had no issue getting involved in an unrelated matter that very same month.

Robert Bruce Hanlon was the Baniszewskis' other next-door neighbor. It was late on the 20th when he noticed some of his belongings were missing from his basement. It did not take him long to figure out who must have stolen them; the Baniszewski children already had a bad reputation on their street and were known for stealing the laundry right off people's clotheslines.

He headed to their front door and knocked angrily. An equally irate Gertrude opened up. Hanlon told her about his missing items and how he knew her roving gang of children had been snooping around his property before. She denied the claim, outraged that anyone would make such an accusation about her parenting. The two bickered on her front porch until Gertrude rushed back inside and called the police.

It did not take long for Gertrude to convince the police to take her side. She argued that it had actually been Hanlon who had been sneaking onto her property, and that she found him in her basement right before she called.

The Vermillions, sitting in their driveway, saw the entire mess play out.

So if Phyllis Vermillion had been the kind of person who kept from sticking her nose in her neighbors' business, she readily set aside that principle when she heard that Hanlon, who was not much older than Gertrude's teenagers, was likely to get almost twenty years in prison for the supposed burglary. She stepped in as a witness for him, set the record straight, and got him freed.

Why had Mrs. Vermillion, who had seen more than enough mistreatment of the girl to make a case against the Baniszewskis, been so reluctant to intervene on Sylvia's behalf? It was a question that she, as well as an entire horrified jury, would be asking for years to come.

XI
More Missed Opportunities

AS FRUSTRATING AS MRS. VERMILLION'S inaction had been, she would not be the only adult who missed their chance to save Sylvia before the final month of her life.

Since his last visit, the Reverend Roy Julian had not stopped worrying about the Baniszewski and Likens girls. Stephanie was still suffering from her random fainting spells, and from the sounds of it, Sylvia was still up to no good. In the middle of the month, he returned to the house to offer more spiritual support.

Once again, Gertrude made sure to monopolize his entire visit. "Sylvia said at school that Paula was going to have a baby, but I know my daughter, and I know Sylvia. Paula is a good girl. She's not going to have a baby—Sylvia is."

"Paula told me that there was some hatred in her heart for Sylvia," he told her.

"Paula is just trying to help me out," Gertrude insisted. "If there is anybody here who is hateful, it's Sylvia."

The Reverend prayed for her again before he left. As worried as he had been for her soul, he did not ask to speak to her this time. He had not seen the girl since she abruptly stopped coming to church. It was a shame; she had been so eager to declare her newfound faith before. Had he insisted on seeing Sylvia, would things have gone differently? Would this well-meaning preacher have been able to save not only her soul, but also her life?

In any case, there was one visitor who had been called to the Baniszewski house to check the health of all the children. The mother of Mike Monroe, one of Sylvia's less-frequent tormentors, had stopped by the Baniszewski house after noticing how often her boy had been going over. She was not the only parent of the neighborhood gang to try to visit, but she was the only one who had gone further inside than the living room. She saw the squalor the nine children were living in—and saw a sad-looking girl whose skin was covered in welts and bruises. Alarmed, she called the authorities.

On the fifteenth, a woman in a white uniform knocked on the front door. Her arrival sent Gertrude into a slight panic, but she always managed to compose herself around important adults.

"Mrs. Wright?"

"Yes. Come in." Gertrude held Dennis Jr. with one arm and gestured inside with the other. "Can I help you?"

Sitting in the living room, Jenny was surprised to see the woman enter. She was Mrs. Sanders, a school nurse. Mrs. Sanders gave her a quick smile before sitting down with Gertrude.

"I'm a public health nurse. I've been called to come talk to you about your children," Mrs. Sanders explained. "May I see them?"

The conversation moved slowly. It was important for the nurse not to jump into the accusations she had heard if she wanted cooperation during her visit. She made sure to ask other important questions first. Inquiring about nutrition and hygiene was the leeway into what had really brought her here.

"Mrs. Wright, have any of your children been sick lately?" she asked.

"No," Gertrude replied with a slight pause. "They have not."

"Well, we received an anonymous phone call stating that there were children here with open sores."

Gertrude must have been feeling the heat on her now. "No. You can check all of my children. Not one of them have any sores on them."

"The woman who called us said she saw a girl with sores all over her body," said the nurse.

Suddenly, Gertrude turned to the girl in the room with them. Jenny was trembling. "Jenny," Gertrude barked. "Go do the dishes!"

Jenny obeyed, just as she had been trained to do so by now, and did not see the nurse again. One can only wonder how the girl must have been feeling as she went into the kitchen, leaving behind someone who had the power to save her ailing sister.

"I know who you're looking for. Jenny's sister, right? Sylvia?" Gertrude leaned in closer to the nurse. Her voice was lower now, almost a whisper. "She has sores all over her body 'cause she won't keep herself clean so I finally had to kick her out of the house."

"Why was that?"

"Why? Because she's a prostitute. That's why. She's not worthy to stay in this house," Gertrude explained. "She runs around with all the boys in the neighborhood."

By now, Paula had joined them on the couch. "That girl is no good," she added.

"She even called my own daughters prostitutes, but I tell you, she's the whore."

Paula nodded along. "Yeah, that girl is no good."

"If it's her you're worried about, we wouldn't know where she is now. She hasn't been here in days," Gertrude was getting annoyed. She stared daggers at the confused nurse. "Who called you, anyway?"

The nurse stood up. If Sylvia was really out somewhere else, there was little reason for Mrs. Sanders to stay. After all, Gertrude was not actually the girl's legal guardian. It was not a crime for her not to know where Sylvia might have run off to. "I don't know. It was an anonymous call. I didn't take it."

Suddenly, the visit was already over. The nurse left and the case was closed.

Jenny must have been filled with regret once Mrs. Sanders left the house, but, terrified as she was, she did make one perilous attempt to stick her neck out for her sister. It was around that same time that she secretly wrote a note detailing all the abuse that Sylvia had suffered at the hands of their caretakers and neighbors alike.

It was a risky move, and she knew it. For over a month now, Jenny had been repeatedly warned that if she was disobedient, whatever they did to Sylvia, they would also do to her. If Gertrude caught Jenny tattling on her, she worried the woman would kill them both.

But things had been out of hand for a long time already. Jenny was afraid that Sylvia wouldn't be able to take much more abuse. Every day, she was growing weaker and weaker. Jenny had to get her out of Gertrude's grasp as soon as possible.

Some way or another, Jenny managed to get a note to their older sister, Dianna. Unfortunately, Dianna was having a hard time believing the outlandish things Jenny had written, and she was already in over her head with her looming divorce. She and her siblings were no strangers to punishment; their parents had been sure to discipline them with a belt plenty of times in the past. Certain her little sister had been exaggerating, Dianna threw the note away as soon as she read it.

Still, something about the note had gotten to her. The details had been so grim, so specific. An innocent girl like Jenny would not have been able to conjure up such horrifying fiction unless there was some small bit of truth to it.

XII

The Basement

JOHN SR. BANISZEWSKI TRIED HIS BEST TO STAY away from his twice-ex-wife, but he loved his children. He gave them what he could; he paid child support when he could afford it, and had given Gertrude an old belt of his to make sure she brought them up right. Now he had something else for them: a puppy.

It wasn't just any puppy, either. This was a police dog sure to keep the family safe once it grew up. He delivered the gift to his gaggle of excited children one October afternoon and was soon on his way.

Gertrude was not pleased at having yet another mouth to feed. Despite his claims that their new pet was a police dog, it was young and untrained. The only thing it would be any good for was making a mess, and the place was filthy enough as it was, Gertrude thought, because of Sylvia.

Like other visitors to the Baniszewski house, the elder John did not venture any deeper than the living room. He did not see the dirt and grime or the lack of food, and even if he had, he would not have seen the most alarming thing in the house, because Gertrude hid that most of all.

Sylvia was down in the basement now, lying naked in the dark. She had been shoved down there by John Sr.'s twice-ex-wife earlier in the month when she could not stop urinating on herself. All those judo flips and stomps to her groin had caused quite a lot of damage to her kidneys, leaving her almost entirely incontinent. According to later testimonies by the younger children, Sylvia had been forbidden from using the bathroom as punishment for wetting herself—though it was not as though Sylvia had a choice. Gertrude had Coy tie her down so that Sylvia could not have gone to the toilet no matter how much she wanted to.

Gertrude flew into a rage the first time she noticed the urine-soaked bed where Sylvia and Jenny slept upstairs. Little Marie Baniszewski, in her continued court testimony, noted that there were not enough beds in the house, and that having one ruined had simply set her mother off. "You don't deserve to sleep upstairs with the human beings," the woman growled as she dragged the listless girl downstairs and pushed her into the dark, damp basement.

Now, she turned her ire at Jenny. The girl watched silently as her sister disappeared down the steps. Gertrude was in her face yelling so loudly that she barely made any sense to Jenny. "Why didn't you call us when this happened, huh?" Gertrude demanded. She gestured towards the door, demanding that Jenny leave. "Get out of there this minute or you'll get some of the same medicine!"

Jenny must have panicked. During these last few months, she had witnessed Sylvia become subject to all kinds of torments, stuff so bad and so wicked that her young mind could have never conceived of it all on her own. The worst thing of all was that she was almost getting used to it by now. She had to if she wanted to stay out of trouble with Gertrude and her minions. After all, hadn't Sylvia herself insisted that Jenny comply with anything the woman demanded of her?

So, she did as she was told, but as she tried to leave the room, Gertrude suddenly had a change of plans. "Why the hell couldn't you wake up? Come on, hurry, damn it—and don't look so stupid. How come you never bothered to wake up? Didn't you feel it for God's sake?"

It never ended. The constant barrage of verbal cruelty, the taunts, the bullying—somehow, Gertrude always had it in her. Even when she was so sick and weak that she could hardly breathe, the woman still managed to spew her hate. Her words moved through the air like some kind of infectious disease that made everyone in the house go crazy. Sunrise to sunset. It was even making Jenny crazy sometimes too.

"I never expected that dirty, lousy Sylvia to wake up. Notice even one fool thing, Monday to Friday. But you shoulda told, Jenny. Cause if you don't tell from now on it's gonna be your fault same as hers."

Jenny apologized. It had become a reflex, something her body just did without her even having to think about it. "Next time," she muttered. "Next time, I'll tell for sure."

"Not gonna be no next time. From now on we're gonna keep that bitch in the basement till she's housebroke. Now you help

Stephanie carry that mattress out into the hall. And look smart and shut up that sniveling or I'll whip you too."

All eyes were on Jenny as she struggled to help Stephanie lift the mattress off the floor. The thing was impossibly heavy. The able-bodied Stephanie was hardly able to keep it upright on her own. Jenny, with her weak leg and her fear, was little help. Finally, she got a proper hold on the mattress by digging her fingernails into its wet surface, and after a few more failed attempts to get it out of the room, she and Stephanie pushed it out into the hall. Later, someone else would throw it down the basement stairs for Sylvia to sleep on.

The puppy was also taken downstairs shortly after John Sr.'s departure, out of Gertrude's sight. In the state Sylvia was in at that point, she probably didn't even notice it.

The only human company she was allowed came when she had gotten so filthy that Gertrude could no longer stand it. Paula, often assisted by Coy Hubbard or Ricky Hobbs or John Jr., would grab Sylvia by the arms and legs and carry her upstairs. Gertrude would have filled the bathtub with scalding hot water in the time it took them to get her to the bathroom.

They would sometimes dunk her in, other times they let the water run over her head and face, and that became their way of treating the festering sores that had opened all over her scalp. Sylvia would cry, but that was not amusing enough for Gertrude.

When the bath was over, Paula and the boys would take turns running salt all over Sylvia's body. It made her scream, which was much more to Gertrude's taste.

On one occasion, Sylvia passed out before the bath was over. Irritated, Gertrude grabbed her by the hair and smashed her face into the side of the tub. She slapped her with all her feeble strength, but it wasn't enough to revive her.

Gertrude took the paddle and smacked Sylvia across the face multiple times. Somehow, this brought the girl back to consciousness. She screamed, and one of the boys rushed to gag her until she could scream no more.

They burned Sylvia with whatever they could: with water, cigarettes, irons. Everything was fair game as long as it hurt her. Afterwards, Gertrude would diligently rub alcohol or other medicine into the girl's wounds. In the woman's mind, this made up for the abuses inflicted on the girl.

Sylvia, who had so rarely gotten to eat an actual meal since she came to stay in that house, was now living on a diet of water and crackers. Sometimes, if her tormentors were feeling especially generous, they would bring down a bowl of soup and allow her to scoop it into her mouth with her hands. If she took too long, they would usually take the soup away.

Among the cruelest tortures involved Sylvia's beloved little sister. Reluctant as she must have been to participate in Gertrude's plans, Jenny gave in. She did it all the time now without complaint. Learning how to shut off her emotions proved to be an invaluable skill in Gertrude's house; it allowed her to blend in, become invisible.

But she could never fully commit to it. There were still times when she risked getting into a world of trouble for helping Sylvia, and though these instances were becoming more and more infrequent, Jenny knew she had to try. At night, after the neighbors had gone home and everyone else had eaten their meager dinners, Jenny would sneak into the basement with scraps of food. Most of the time, the best she could do was crackers. Once, she had tried to save her own dinner for Sylvia, but that was not an easy feat when there was only one spoon left that they all had to take turns using.

Did Gertrude ever catch on to these clandestine visits to the basement? One could only imagine her rage. All the blame would have been placed on Sylvia's shoulders, of course; Gertrude always went on and on about how greedy the girl was, so sneaky and manipulative. "Pig" was just one of the many insults Gertrude hurled at her on a daily basis. Jenny would not be able to escape punishment this time, either.

The memory of that first bad day, the aftermath of a late payment, was still fresh in her mind. Jenny remembered being taken upstairs with her sister and then both of them told to lean forward on the bed. Their underwear pulled down. The wood of the paddle stung their bare flesh with every hit. *I took care of you two bitches for nothing!* Gertrude's voice rose over their cries. Who knew a woman so sickly had it in her?

Smacks on the ass were easy. They were perhaps too easy now that Gertrude had done so much worse.

Those crackers. If Jenny was going to waste what little food the family had on her no-good sister, Gertrude figured she might as well use that to her advantage. What happened next was later told in court by Jenny herself:

"I went back upstairs and Gerty told me to tell Sylvia she could have another chance, that she could have a cracker and see if she would take it and some water. Shirley got a cup of water and I got a cracker and Sylvia said, 'I don't want it, give it to the dog. It is hungrier than I am.' I said, 'I know that you are hungry.' She said she did not want it. I knew she would get in trouble. Shirley put the water in her mouth and Sylvia drank it. Shirley ran to her mother and said she drank the water. She could not force it away because her hands were tied. Gerty comes to the basement and said,' You know you were not supposed to have water.' Sylvia said, 'I did not want it but Shirley made me drink it.' Gerty took her fist and kept hitting her in the stomach."

A dirty trick. Sylvia seemed to know this right away. She would be punished for taking the forbidden food, and she would be punished for refusing this rare display of generosity from Gertrude. So why would Jenny have complied? The younger girl stated that she had simply gone downstairs to spend time with her sister, an innocent and routine visit. After all, she had been in pain since one of the boys tied her up again. Gertrude saw an opportunity to break both girls and took it.

There seemed to be no limits to the depravity Sylvia was subjected to. Sometime during the final week of Sylvia's life,

Gertrude got a particularly diabolical idea. She recalled how "greedy" Sylvia had been back in August, eating an entire sandwich in the park while the Baniszewskis children were forced to go hungry, and realized she had never properly punished the girl for that. While she stood in the basement, she called for Johnny. "Go get some shit," ordered.

He promptly brought back one of Dennis Jr.'s loaded diapers and shoved its contents into Sylvia's mouth. Then he replaced Sylvia's small water supply with a cup full of urine. When the girl could not consume the waste, they simply smeared the diaper and urine all over her face. When the ordeal was over, she was "rewarded" with half a cup of water. It was all she was allowed to have for the entire day.

There was probably some small part of her that missed the noxious hot dog from months before—including that second helping.

Sylvia was gravely ill by now, and her incontinence was growing worse. It came as a surprise to her when Gertrude gave her yet another "second chance" at living upstairs among the rest of them. All she had to do was make it through a single night without wetting the bed. Of course, there was one small catch:

Sylvia would have to hold it in. She would not be allowed to go to the bathroom. To ensure this, Gertrude had Sylvia's limbs tied to the bedposts.

It was not as though Sylvia did not try, but she was going delirious with malnutrition by that point. She still would not be allowed food, but Jenny could get away with bringing her a little water. A reckless idea perhaps, but who could blame a starving child for wanting anything that may satiate the pain in her belly?

The following morning, the bed was stained with urine, and Gertrude promptly threw Sylvia back down into the basement.

Her punishment this time involved another show with a glass soda bottle.

XIII

The Tattoo

IT IS UNCLEAR HOW OR WHEN EXACTLY fourteen-year-old Richard Hobbs started coming over to the Baniszewski house. Known by everyone as Ricky, the boy was about as rambunctious as the rest of the gang, despite the strict moral teachings he so often received from his disciplinarian father, Woodrow Hobbs. But the boy was not exactly a friend to Paula, Stephanie, or even Johnny. Later on, in front of the police, the boy would specify that his friend in the house was Gertrude.

That season was not the dusk of life for Sylvia only, for in a nearby hospital, Ricky's mother, Juanita, was losing her battle with cancer. With a terminally ill mother, a gaggle of siblings, and a father so often away at work, Ricky turned to Gertrude. Indeed, the boy was one of the Baniszewskis' most frequent visitors, stopping by once, sometimes twice a day after school.

Given the circumstances of Ricky's own family life, one might have expected that his attachment to Gertrude was rooted in some yearning for a mother figure. However, the truth was quite a bit more scandalous.

Gertrude liked her men young. It was easier for her to sink her claws in an inexperienced youth than it was a grown man. An older woman willing to put out was a siren call to the curious and unsuspecting. It had been how she kept Dennis Wright at her side for as long as she did, but she made plenty of mistakes with him.

Her former common-law husband was an adult, and he had known women before her. On the other hand, Ricky Hobbs had never even had a girlfriend.

It is unknown what exactly, if anything, Gertrude did with Ricky. What is known is that she performed a strip tease for the boy on at least one occasion and that Ricky was ready and willing to do anything Gertrude asked of him. "This is just like how they do it at the Fox Theatre downtown," she reportedly said as she unbuttoned her blouse for Ricky and Coy one afternoon. She bared her bra and bony stomach as she danced around the room.

During the weekend right before Sylvia's death, Gertrude went across town for a doctor's visit. When she came home, Ricky was already there. Gertrude was glad to see him; she had come up with a new game in the short time she had been away that morning.

When Gertrude called for Sylvia to come upstairs, Ricky was stunned to see her in such a terrible state. It was a wonder that the girl, whose body was covered all over with burns and bruises, could even climb up the steps on her own.

"Do you know how to put on a tattoo, Ricky?" Gertrude asked.

"Yeah," the boy replied. "I guess so."

The woman turned her hateful gaze to Sylvia. "Do you know what a tattoo is, Sylvia?"

"Yes, ma'am." Sylvia's voice was hoarse and weak, practically a whisper.

That was when Marie came over. She handed her mother a sewing needle.

"Well then," said Gertrude, holding the needle up to the light. She lit a match under it and let the metal heat up. "You have branded my daughters, so now I'm going to brand you." She looked back over to Ricky. "She's a prostitute, and she's proud of it, so we'll put that on her stomach."

Next, she ordered Sylvia to undress. When the girl was unable to strip down quickly enough, Gertrude practically tore her soiled clothing off. She took a seat in front of her and carved the word "I" right on her flesh.

Jenny watched as Sylvia writhed in pain. The older girl gritted her teeth and shook her head from side to side, but she did not scream.

As for the rest of the sentence, she let Ricky have the honor. She made mention of feeling ill before handing the boy the needle.

"Wait," he asked her. "How do you spell prostitute?"

Gertrude wrote down the word for him before heading to her room. It seemed that the ordeal had worn her out already, despite how excited she seemed about it. Before she went to bed, she told

Jenny to run an errand, something she tended to do when she did not want Jenny to see what was done to Sylvia.

The younger girl's spirit had been thoroughly broken, and she did not dare to disobey Gertrude. Jenny did as she was told and headed to the local grocery store with just enough money in her pocket to buy a loaf of bread. She went as fast as she could. Helpless as she was, she still never liked leaving Sylvia alone in there with those people.

With Jenny gone, Ricky saw the chance to make the branding a little extra fun. He took another match and held it to the tip of the needle, partly to sterilize it and partly to keep making the branding painful as possible for Sylvia.

But Sylvia was doing so poorly that she did not cry or scream. She was too dehydrated by that point to produce tears. As Ricky carved the message into her skin, she could only clench her teeth. Ricky grew annoyed when she moved too much and smacked her a couple of times on her chest.

Jenny returned from the store less than a half hour later and headed towards the kitchen. It was rather crowded in the room; Gertrude, Paula, Johnny, Shirley, and Marie were all seated at the table, as though they had been waiting for her. Beyond this room, she saw Ricky still standing over Sylvia with the sewing needle in his hand.

Sylvia got a brief reprieve from the humiliation when Randy Lepper arrived. Gertrude thought it too scandalous to have the twelve-year-old Randy see Sylvia naked again, so she ordered Ricky, Jenny, and Marie to send her back downstairs and dress her.

Ricky found an iron poker and got an even better idea. He asked Marie to heat it up like they had the needle, but the flame was too small. That was when the little girl decided to use the furnace to light up some paper, and this worked well enough.

They soon brought Sylvia back upstairs to show Randy their handiwork. The younger boy, who had not been over to the Baniszewskis as often, was a bit confused about Sylvia's countless wounds.

"What happened to her?" he asked.

Gertrude sneered. "She just got back from a sex party."

Randy found it funny. He always laughed when they did bad things to Sylvia. He would still be laughing at the memories of her torture several months later in front of a judge, but for now, he was losing interest and decided to head home.

The branding continued shortly after Randy left. This time, Shirley replaced Marie as Ricky's assistant. They got the idea to brand an S for Sylvia right above the crass message, and decided that heating up a crowbar would be the easiest way to do it.

The crowbar had one end shaped like a semi-circle. Applied twice, it would form an S. However, Shirley got confused and applied the bar incorrectly when her turn came. The S ended up being an ugly, red number three.

In any case, Gertrude was delighted with the result. "Look at you, Sylvia," she said in between laughs. "What are you gonna do now? You know you can't get married."

"That is right," Sylvia replied.

Gertrude laughed. "You can't undress in front of a husband or anyone because that'll be on your stomach. No man is going to want you anymore. What are you going to do?"

Sylvia could only shrug in response. "There is nothing I can do. It is there now."

"You're proud of it," Gertrude asked. "Aren't you?"

"No," she replied weakly.

Later that day, Sylvia received her typical abuse in the form of beatings from Coy and Paula before she was allowed to go to bed. Jenny, desperately worried now, decided to risk getting punished herself and went downstairs to spend some time with her sister. They were seeing less and less of each other now. Gertrude hated seeing them together and was always trying to keep them apart.

How much longer were they meant to endure this? When were their parents going to come back? Did it even matter if they did? It wasn't as though Lester and Betty had never visited. They had come to Gertrude's house numerous times over the past few months, and everyone acted like everything was normal and Sylvia wasn't going through hell every single day for no reason. How didn't they see, they wondered. How didn't they see how thin and scared they were, how fake their smiles were and how they forced their laughter was? Or their obvious hunger? Sylvia's pale skin and black eyes?

But it wasn't fair to put all the blame on their parents. Lots of grownups had come to the house, and nobody noticed. Gertrude described the sisters—little bitches, she had called them, cheap and dirty girls.

Jenny watched her sister shift slightly on the dirty mattress the way one would when they were trying to get more comfortable. She looked at the branding on her sister's stomach and wondered if such a thing as comfort still existed for Sylvia. It might have been more useful to take her mind off their reality.

Happy memories. There was always something good in between all the bad, even now. Jenny remembered the start of the year, how it couldn't be more different than now because they were living all the way across the country in sunny Long Beach, California. It was only for a few months, but hadn't it been so much fun?

Did Sylvia remember the boy she had met there? Of course. She must have. He had been her first boyfriend—well, her first *almost* boyfriend.

The sisters giggled.

California was a whole different world than Indiana. It was warm, even when they first arrived in January of 1965. They had been there in the springtime, maybe until May. Yes, it was May when they left. They knew because they remembered celebrating Easter with a couple of girls they had befriended, and they had all put on their best dresses and took a picture in front of a church together.

It seemed so long ago, like it was somebody else's life. Where was that picture now? Maybe seeing it would cheer Sylvia up. Or maybe it would just make things worse.

Jenny could not help but wonder where their California friends were now. Did those girls ever think about them? Did that boy miss Sylvia?

That boy. Gertrude had gotten so mad when Sylvia talked about him that single time. Now everyone thought Sylvia was a whore because Gertrude got the wrong idea. Now any memories with that boy would be tainted forever, turned ugly and shameful.

Gertrude made it sound like it was a sin for Sylvia to be happy, like it was a sin for her to feel anything other than shame. Sylvia stirred again. Her movements had been getting slower and her breathing more labored.

"Jenny," Sylvia spoke feebly. "I know you don't want me to die, but I'm gonna die. I can tell."

Panic rose in Jenny's chest. This was the first time Sylvia had said anything so scary. She hadn't even liked talking about her pain before back before it had gotten so bad. The thought that she could give up made Jenny want to cry.

"Well, don't die," said Jenny softly. "Please."

XIV

The End Comes

GERTRUDE WAS GETTING ANXIOUS. THE dynamic within the house was changing. It was slow, but it was so obvious that even the kids were noticing it. Sylvia was slipping away—not just physically, but mentally too.

Later, one of the neighborhood boys would go on to say that the torture was getting boring by that point. Sylvia was now so weak that she could hardly react to what they did anymore. One of the few things that amused them now was "treating" her wounds. Some of the kids had made such a fuss about those open, puss-filled sores on Sylvia's head getting infected that Gertrude finally did something about it. In one of the upstairs bedrooms, she and Paula took turns pouring rubbing alcohol into Sylvia's wounds, and when they ran out of alcohol, they rubbed salt in the cuts on her legs and knees.

It was fun to make the girl scream again. The pain was bad enough to make Sylvia pass out and remained unconscious for most of her "treatment." That was what they told Jenny, at least.

But even that got old before long.

If Gertrude had ever really hoped to kill Sylvia, she had not expected the end to come so quickly. On October 24th leading into the 25th—the day before Sylvia's death—the woman was trying frantically to think of a plan. Sylvia had just made a rare attempt to escape, but she was so weak by then that Gertrude had no trouble stopping her. It meant that Sylvia knew something bad would happen soon, and Gertrude knew it too.

In fact, it had originally been Gertrude's idea to get Sylvia out of the house and be rid of her for good. It was something that she had been considering as an option for some time, but as Sylvia grew weaker and weaker, she decided it was time to put that plan into action.

And why would she not want to get rid of the girl? After all, Sylvia was getting on her last nerve. When she was not holding out on them by staying silent during torture sessions, she was crying and screaming her head off. No doubt the Vermillions next door would start getting suspicious again, causing her even more trouble.

According to later testimony, there were actually two attempts made to get rid of Sylvia. Details about the first trip outside are scant, though Jenny believes it happened in the evening three or four days prior to the end. Gertrude ordered Jenny to head upstairs. The girl went, but not before she overheard part of Gertrude's conversation with Johnny. She was telling her son to take Sylvia out somewhere where he could lose her, like an alleyway or a street a good distance from the house.

Johnny did indeed leave with Sylvia, but to his mother's annoyance, he did not come back alone. Sylvia, who was in a disoriented, almost zombielike state, had somehow managed to follow him. She was, unsurprisingly, punished for it.

More trouble. More unnecessary stress. Gertrude's health was bad enough without Sylvia causing her constant headaches, so when she later found some soiled rags in the house, she demanded the girl show herself. This was the second attempt.

"I'm right here, Gertie," said Sylvia, her voice weak. It was coming from down in the basement, the place where she was kept almost all the time now. She was tied to the mattress as punishment for some arbitrary thing she had done earlier. "No, it wasn't me. I didn't wet the rags. Can I go to the bathroom now?"

This enraged Gertrude. Even someone like Sylvia should have known better than to ask such a stupid question. Sylvia had been forbidden from using the bathroom as a punishment for soiling the mattress. It had been decided that she was unworthy of using the toilet upstairs until she proved she could hold it in—a losing battle. Now she had urinated all over some more of Gertrude's belongings and had the gall to try and weasel her way out of the basement?

Gertrude called Jenny over. It was getting late, and the younger girl was already in her pajamas. That hardly mattered to Gertrude. "Go upstairs and get dressed," she ordered. "You and Johnny are going to blindfold Sylvia and then you're going to take her over to Jimmy's woods and lose her."

Jenny approached the scene timidly. Gertrude handed her a piece of cloth and said she was going to wrap it around her sister's head as soon as they got her upstairs. Johnny was already down there undoing the ropes.

It was a risky move, but Gertrude knew it would be much harder to implicate her if Sylvia was found dead in the wilderness than in the house—this is despite the fact that Jimmy's woods, located within a few miles of East New York Street, was said to have more closely resembled a vacant lot than an actual forest. In an attempt to cover all her bases, she had Sylvia, still conscious but just barely, write a note detailing a story of misadventure.

They did not let Sylvia in on their plan, but she had overheard enough—how could she not have, with the way Gertrude was always yelling? She understood that they wanted to leave her to die out there all alone. It was a terrifying prospect, even after everything she had endured here, and she could not let it happen.

If they wanted to get rid of her so badly, so be it then. Mustering up what little strength she still had, Sylvia rose to her feet and limped as fast as she could to the front door, towards freedom. Where would she go? That did not matter. All that mattered was that she crossed the threshold from this hell to the world beyond. Once she made it to the streets, then she could think about it. She could cry for help or go to a neighbor's house. Maybe she could go to Arsenal Tech and find a teacher. She could find Dianna. She could wander the streets downtown. It did not matter.

All that mattered was that she get away from all these horrible people.

For a moment, it left everyone shocked. She still had some sense of self-preservation, after all.

Sylvia fumbled through the front door. She made it to the porch, the evening air cold against her skin.

Before she could take another step, Gertrude yanked her back by the air. "Get back! You ain't going anywhere!" she screamed. She took hold of Sylvia's arm and, as weak as she was, managed to pull her inside the house with such force that Sylvia was half-dragged along the ground.

But why? Why would Gertrude force her to stay when just a minute ago she had been so eager to kick her out? She hated Sylvia so much that the thought of giving in to her, allowing her the dignity of dying on her own terms, was unacceptable. If Sylvia wanted to go out, then Gertrude forbade it. It was only a good idea back when she thought it scared the girl.

How dare she? Gertrude was fuming mad. How dare Sylvia try to trick her, try to play helpless and sick and then try to get loose? Forget getting rid of her; there was no way that Gertrude was letting the little brat take the easy way out.

Perhaps she could keep the girl from dying a little longer if she finally gave her something to eat. Then she could figure something else out. After pulling her into the kitchen and sitting her at the table, she made Sylvia two pieces of toast. Sylvia brought the toast to her swollen lips and tried to chew once or twice, but then her mouth just hung open. The mushy food fell out. "I can't swallow," said Sylvia.

This ungrateful brat. How dare she refuse this act of generosity? Frustrated, Gertrude took a metal curtain rod off the wall and beat Sylvia across the face until the it bent at both ends. Sylvia did not cry again this time. She only slumped over in her seat.

Sylvia mumbled, but a combination of dizziness and mouth trauma made it difficult to understand her.

The kitchen looked different all of a sudden. Was it always this dark? Someone should turn the lights on.

The evening of the 24th was marked by a visit from Coy Hubbard. He had swung by to get in some more "judo practice" after work, though his training session somehow involved knocking Sylvia unconscious with a broom.

This went well on into the night.

"I am going to get you out of my house!" yelled Gertrude. "You are going to get the hell out of my house!"

Somehow, Sylvia, who had been brought up from the basement, was still able to stand. She looked at Jenny. "It's getting dark…" she said. "I can't see anything. It's all turning black. Everything."

Then she collapsed.

"Get me some hot water!" Gertrude shouted. "Some hot water'll wake this bitch right up."

That command was aimed at her, Jenny knew, but she did not move. She could not move even if she wanted to. All she could do was watch Sylvia writhing on the floor, her sister's eyes fluttering half open and shut as though her eyelids were too heavy. Her arms reached blindly around as she tried to push herself back up. Even now, even as she was dying, she was still trying to obey Gertrude—but it was no use. She kept slipping back onto the floor.

Gertrude got the hot water herself. She stood over Sylvia and dumped a cup full over the girl's face, startling her enough that she almost managed to get back up on her feet.

Almost. Despite her best effort, Sylvia simply did not have the strength to stand anymore. Her legs gave out and she fell again, her head hitting Jenny's bad foot.

It's black. It's all going black…

Gertrude dragged Sylvia back onto a chair and found her favorite wooden paddle. She swung but missed when the girl fell over again, and the momentum made it so Gertrude hit herself in the face. The pain left her dazed for a moment. "I think my jaw is broken," she said to herself.

Enraged and embarrassed, Gertrude told Jenny to go to bed and not come out until morning, but before that she had to fetch Paula for her. Hesitant, Jenny moved slowly towards the staircase.

A feeling of total helplessness weighed her down. The last thing she wanted was to leave Sylvia with Gertrude while she was in such a bad state—but she did it. It would be something she would come to regret for the rest of her life.

It was after midnight when Jenny got to bed. Whatever Gertrude and Paula were doing to Sylvia went on for a couple more hours.

On the morning of the 25th, Jenny tried to feed her sister with similar results. Sylvia had been starving for so long that her body was rejecting food. Her mouth was swollen from abuse, and her lips chewed up. It was a struggle to even get water into her mouth.

It must be getting late. It looks like nighttime inside this room. The whole place looks so dark and cold and empty, like a bad dream. Why won't anyone turn the lights on?

When Gertrude's two attempts to feed Sylvia milk also failed, she stomped over the girl's face and decided it was time for a different approach. If the girl was going to die under her roof, all Gertrude could do now was direct the blame somewhere else.

But first, she figured she ought to get Sylvia cleaned up. With no control over her bowels, the girl was living in her own waste. Johnny undressed her, and then Gertrude covered Sylvia's limp body with laundry detergent and dishwashing soap. Using a garden house borrowed from the Lepper family, they attempted to wash the grime off Sylvia.

It's so dark.

Stephanie arrived that evening and was appalled by the scene. She shut the hose off and tried to carry her upstairs for a proper bath but found herself unable to bear the girl's weight on her own.

Mother and daughter began to panic. Sylvia stopped moving. She was completely unresponsive. Stephanie could not detect her breathing anymore.

Ricky Hobbs found both of them weeping when he came over to visit a short while later. They were relieved when he managed to detect very faint breathing. Stephanie ordered Johnny to go run a warm bath upstairs while she and Ricky brought Sylvia up.

Sylvia's wet body slipped from Ricky's grasp, and her head banged on the basement steps, rending her almost unconscious again.

Meanwhile, Gertrude was following behind them, growing hysterical. "She's faking it!"

They shut Gertrude out of the bathroom and let Sylvia rest for a while in the warm water. She had opened her eyes a little and was struggling to stay awake. "I… I wish my daddy was here," she moaned. Stephanie brushed her hair back and let her cry.

They wrapped her up in a warm blanket when the bath was over and lay her on a bed.

"She's a faker! She's faking it," Gertrude shrieked from outside the room. She barged in, a book in her hand, and threw it at Sylvia's head. "Look! She's fine! Faker!"

"Get out!" Stephanie cried. Ricky managed to wrangle her back outside.

Sylvia's tired puffy eyes met Stephanie's again. She gave a soft whimper. "Oh, Stephanie, take me home."

Her breathing stopped entirely. It was finally over.

XV
A Shocking Scene

IT WAS RICKY HOBBS WHO CALLED THE POLICE. Since there was no telephone in the Baniszewski house, they were forced to hurry down to the closest gas station to use theirs. The widespread implementation of 911 as an emergency was still years away, so it was difficult to tell when help would arrive. If they were hoping there was anything that could still be done for Sylvia at that point, they were left disappointed.

By the time the police arrived at the Baniszewski house, Sylvia was dead.

Officer Melvin Dixon had been one of the first officers to arrive at the scene. He had gotten the call on his patrol car's radio just before seven in the evening, at the tail end of what had otherwise been an uneventful day. "Investigate possible dead girl," was all the report said. The lack of context led Dixon to believe that a terrible accident had taken place. Nothing could prepare him for the crime scene he would find instead.

When Dixon asked what happened, Gertrude put on the face of a concerned caregiver and recounted Sylvia's supposed wild excursions and her fondness for orgies and "sex parties." In her version of events, Sylvia had taken off with a group of juvenile delinquents. After they had their fun with her, they dumped her back into Gertrude's yard.

Sylvia came to Gertrude badly beaten and half-naked, her scarred breasts exposed. Before succumbing to her injuries, the girl handed her caregiver a note addressed to her parents:

"*Mr. and Mrs. Likens,*

I went with a gang of boys in the middle of the night. And they said that they would pay me if I would give them something so I got in the car and they all got what they wanted and they did and did and when they got finished they beat me up and left sores on my face and all over my body.

And they also put on my stomach, I am a prostitute and proud of it.

I have done just about everything that I could do just to make Gertie mad and cause cost Gertie more money than she's got. I've tore up a new mattress and peaed (sic) on it. I have also cost Gertie doctor bills that she really can't pay and made Gertie a nervous wreck and all her kids. I cost her $35.00 for a hospital in one day and I wouldn't do nothing around the house. I have done anything to do things to make things out of the way to make things worse for them."

Odd as it was, it was all the police had to go on at that moment. That everyone in the house corroborated Gertrude's story only made it more believable. Besides, who else besides criminals would be capable of inflicting such brutality on a teenage girl? The cops were, at that moment, far more concerned with getting to the victim. They hardly had the time to look over all the small, bizarre details from the note such as the lack of a signature as well as the fact that Sylvia referred to her own parents so formally.

A world away from the horrors of East New York Street, Dr. Arthur Paul Keber chatted among his fellow members of the state's high society after dinner. It was a small but pleasant gathering held in a hotel on October 26th that was suddenly interrupted by a bellboy shortly before eight that evening. The bellboy informed Dr. Kebel about a message from the Medical Society exchange board. They were in need of his expertise—a crime had occurred in a house that was located in a bad neighborhood.

Dr. Kebel, the deputy coroner of Indianapolis, arrived at the scene about an hour later. The atmosphere of the house was immediately heavy, thick with tension and dread. Once the officers finished taking pictures of the scene, Dr. Kebel headed towards the scene of the crime itself. There had been mention of the basement, but he was directed upstairs to one of the bedrooms

The doctor was no stranger to sights of violence. He was a coroner, and before that, he had been a 2nd Lieutenant in the U.S. Army during the second World War. He knew death, understood it well, but though he had been clued in on what occurred in the Baniszewski house, nothing could have prepared him for the horrific sight that awaited him in that room.

In the dark, grim room was a mattress leaning against the wall. A bony girl had been placed on top, seemingly carelessly because half of her body was hanging off.

Dr. Kebel stepped closer. A strong, foul smell burned his nose, and he realized that the mattress had been soiled, soaked with urine in several spots and caked with feces. Some of the fluids seemed to have been there for a while as they left stains that had crusted over. A dog, he understood, had been kept within this house, but these living conditions were not suitable for an animal.

They were certainly not suitable for a human being, for the girl who lay before him, dead.

"When I first saw her," Dr. Kebel later recounted in court. "Her hands were folded across her chest."

Before any sort of examination could begin, he made sure to get a good look at the girl's face. It was important that he could recognize her later in photographs—something likely easier said than done given the condition she was in. It could be difficult to match such battered features to a photo of a still-living person.

He would be the first professional to touch the body. It was evident that she had been handled and moved by others following her time of death. This was for a few reasons.

The first was the attire. She was clad in a pair of white pedal-pusher pants and a blouse. The doctor noted that her hair was damp, and though her surroundings were filthy, Sylvia herself was not. "The clothes were surprisingly clean in contrast to other surroundings in the room," he further explained. "The clothes looked fresh like they had been recently laundered and put on this person."

An important distinction. Sylvia had been *dressed*. She had not dressed herself.

The second reason was the pose. It was also unlikely that she had died in the position she had been found half-off the mattress with her hands crossed over her chest, eerily reminiscent of a body in a casket. This appeared to have been a strategic move; when the girl's hands were moved aside and the blouse lifted, it gave investigators a full view of her emaciated torso. A shockingly degrading claim had been carved onto her skin.

I AM A PROSTITUTE AND PROUD OF IT

Kebel had known from the first look that the injuries were numerous, and he would have to examine every single one, but that task came after he estimated the time of her death. He carefully picked up the body, and was immediately struck by how light it was. She was quite thin, but it seemed like she weighed next to nothing.

Her limbs were stiff, completely stiff. He noted that, when the body was lifted, it did not "break at the hips," staying instead completely flat. Rigor mortis had fully set in. Next, he checked her body's temperature and found it lacking all warmth. The abdomen was typically among the last parts of the body to get cold, but the girl's skin was at room temperature all over.

She had been dead a while. A couple of hours at least, he figured.

Kebel continued his examination, making note of all the marks that covered Sylvia's entire body. In other cases, doing so was a relatively straightforward process; many of the dead people he saw were shot, stabbed, hit by cars. These were terrible ways to die, of course, but these were forms of violence that he could understand, that he could wrap his head around.

What he saw on the body puzzled him. There were more marks than he could count during this initial look. He would uncover everything else after the body was transported to Marion County General Hospital and an autopsy was performed. Here are just some of his findings:

He found several cuts and bruises, including a large one along the right side her head near the temple that looked fresh, lesions on her cheeks and jaw, patches of her skin that had been eroded, likely by hot water, though he noted that a caustic substance such as toilet bowl cleanser could also have been used, damage to her vagina, notably the labia, which left it swollen and "extremely puffy," and over one hundred puncture wounds over her entire body, some so deep they were nearly to the bone.

He concluded that this was not simply the work of common criminals; this had to have been the work of a madman. Whoever it was, he knew they must have been a very dangerous person.

Kebel's train of thought was interrupted when left the bedroom and was approached by the lady of the house, a tense-looking woman who the police had referred to as Mrs. Wright. She brought him down to the living room, perhaps to ask about what he had seen, but he beat her to the questions.

"Was this child under your care?" he asked.

"Yes," she replied.

"Well then, I must ask why you did not call for help earlier. You should have called a doctor, at least."

"Didn't think I needed to. I ain't got a lot of money, you see. Besides," she explained. "I was already treating the girl myself—I even bought a couple of first aid supplies for her."

"You did?"

She nodded. "Yes, sir. I put some alcohol and medication on her."

Kebel thought about it for a moment. The cuts and lesions had all appeared clean, even the fresher ones. There was no oozing blood, but there was no sign of ointment or medication, either. It would have made sense, he supposed, if she had been bathed recently, though that did not make it any less frustrating to know that evidence had possibly been washed away.

"What about the black eye?" he asked. "Do you know where she got that?"

Dr. Kebel would later recall that, while Mrs. Wright did offer a response to this last question, he had unfortunately failed to commit her answer to memory. It was possible that he did not consider what she was saying to have been terribly important. He found the woman strange; she was clearly high strung and somewhat thoughtless if she had let this poor girl suffer without proper help, but there was still no reason to suspect anything else. At this point, he and law enforcement were still working under the belief that Sylvia had died at the hands of a gang of boys.

As he left the Baniszewski home, he assumed that this was the last he would see of Mrs. Wright and her children. He would be wrong. By then, Jenny, who had been raking leaves for neighbors, had already returned to the house. She was distraught and anxious. Some police officers were still present at the scene, and someone had already informed her of her sister's sad fate.

Not long after, Paula came home and heard the news. "You're kidding!" she said.

Paula went and grabbed her bible. Before Jenny could react further, Paula took her hand. "This was meant to happen," she told her. "If you want to live with us, Jenny, we'll treat you like our own sister."

Jenny managed to hold it together during some brief questioning. Gertrude had come into the room and Jenny was still too frightened of her to contradict the woman's story. She maintained that her sister had run off with some boys and went missing for days, only to return when she was on the brink of death.

When the cops were preparing to leave, however, one of them felt a tug at their sleeve. Jenny looked up at him with sad, wide eyes. "Get me out of here," she whispered. "And I'll tell you everything."

The police managed to find Dianna's address. That was where Jenny would stay until they could contact her parents.

As for Mr. and Mrs. Likens, they had received that dreadful phone call while they were fast asleep in their hotel room down in Florida. They had to borrow money from a friend to afford the plane ticket back to Indiana. They wept when they arrived at the police station to identify Sylvia's mutilated body.

The next few days saw Sylvia's funeral, and the next few months would see a criminal trial unlike any the state of Indiana had seen before.

XVI

The Truth Comes Out

DR. CHARLES R. ELLIS HAD SEEN SOME TERRIBLE things in his career. With nearly three hundred criminal autopsies under his belt, the young pathologist was well-acquainted with the effects of violence on the human body. Yet the body of this murdered teenager was like nothing he had ever seen before. In terms of sheer brutality, this case was in a class of its own.

Along with the cuts, burns, bruises, and puncture wounds that had been previously noted by Dr. Kebel, there was more disturbing injuries uncovered during the autopsy. The state of her lips was of particular interest. Ellis would recount the details in court:

"…examining the lips, the lips were markedly torn and essentially in shreds, except the lip directly under where the right front tooth would be. This tooth was absent. That was the only place where the lips were not shredded…. These tearing or laceration of the lip extended through from the outer surface to the inner surface, completely through in some areas. It indicated to me that the deceased had been chewing on her lip."

Sylvia had been missing that upper-right tooth since she was a small child. She had been playfighting with her little brother Benny, Jenny's twin, and her tooth was knocked out by accident. The gap in her teeth became an insecurity for her as she grew up, affecting the way she smiled. A careful, tight-lipped grin became one of her most identifiable quirks.

Nearly all of her fingernails had been bent backwards, likely done in a frantic attempt to claw at something—or at herself. The only exception was her middle fingernail on her left hand. This one had been ripped clean off.

Malnutrition was evident even before Dr. Ellis could make a single incision. She had lost so much weight that her bones, particularly her pelvis, were prominent. The liver was visibly damaged from malnutrition and had turned yellow. Other organs, such as her kidneys and brain, were also in a bad state.

Her vagina was still red and inflamed, though it was determined that she had not been sexually abused since no sperm was recovered and "no entrance" had occurred. Ellis found a large hematoma—a gathering of blood that collected within tissue outside of blood vessels on her left labia, an injury that suggested blunt force trauma to the genitals. The incident with the soda bottle had not yet come to light. She was, of course, not pregnant.

Ultimately, it was determined that her cause of death was a subdural hematoma; a build-up of blood within the skull and around the brain caused by head trauma leading to increased intracranial pressure. It had become obvious to him the moment he had removed the top of the skull and saw a massive bruise on the left side of the brain. Ellis noted that the blood appeared to have been of a "fresh nature, unclotted, still of rather red color…", meaning that the decedent had likely received this injury two to three days before her death.

Underlying factors such as shock from her numerous injuries and malnutrition had also likely contributed to the decedent's death.

Elsewhere, law enforcement was finally catching up on the truth thanks to Jenny's whispered plea. Ricky Hobbs, who had already gone to bed, was awoken by police and taken down to their headquarters to join Gertrude. Meanwhile, all of the Baniszewski children were taken to a juvenile center where they would remain in custody during the trial.

Without Gertrude's manipulation, Ricky was more forthcoming with the truth. He admitted to being a friend of Gertrude's and having taken part in the tattooing, branding, and some of the beatings. He had done those things because he had been told to do so, he claimed, and he only did it because Gertrude was a trusted adult, so she had to have known what was best.

It became clear that Gertrude was more involved than she initially led law enforcement to believe. While they questioned her, they had Ricky transferred to the detention ward of a local hospital due to his diabetes. There, he would spend the majority of his time for the next several months chained to his bed, allowed out only for rare occasions such as visiting his dying mother and later attending her funeral. Juanita Hobbs passed away never knowing about her son's criminal activities.

While Ricky, pressured by his father Woodrow Hobbs, was more honest, Gertrude only continued to deny any involvement. First, she tried her usual methods to build up sympathy. She claimed she had been too sick and weak to know exactly what the kids had really been doing with Sylvia. Then, she said that she knew what was happening but was too weak to partake in the abuse or put a stop to it, but she had tried to "doctor" Sylvia by rubbing alcohol on her wounds. Reluctantly, she admitted that she made Sylvia sleep in the basement because she kept urinating the bed at night, and once she told Johnny to "go get some shit and make her eat it."

Finally, when nothing else seemed to be working, she implicated Paula and Coy Hubbard.

Coy, who was not known to police at all before this, was quickly arrested while at school the following day.

In juvie, Paula made a written confession about her involvement. She admitted to hitting Sylvia with the police belt and hitting her in the jaw so hard she broke her own wrist. Johnny made similar confessions, but he also made a list of the other neighborhood children who had been involved with Sylvia's torture.

On October 28, 1965, the day before Sylvia's funeral, police arrested Anna Siscoe and Mike Monroe. The next day, they arrested Judy Duke and Randy Lepper.

What had first looked like a case of gang violence was quickly becoming one of the most unusual homicide cases the state had ever seen.

The case gained media attention due to the number of unlikely suspects involved. Throughout November and December, the newspaper *The Indianapolis Star* reported on court proceedings. Several charges were leveled against the main suspects including first and second degree murder, voluntary and involuntary manslaughter, assault and battery in the attempt to gratify sexual desires, assault and battery with the intent to kill, rape, sodomize, and commit forgery.

Stephanie's attorney, John R. Hammond, tried to get any murder charges levied at Stephanie dismissed but was unsuccessful, though the girl did agree to testify against the others.

Facing first degree murder charges were: Gertrude (Mrs. Wright) Baniszewski, Paula Marie Baniszewski, Stephanie Kay Baniszewski, John (Johnny) Baniszewski Jr., Coy Hubbard, and Richard (Ricky) Dean Hobbs.

In Indiana, at the time, a conviction of first degree murder meant the death penalty.

XVII

The Truth Comes Out

GERTRUDE'S YOUNGEST CHILDREN WERE TAKEN into state care and put in foster homes for the meantime. The other neighborhood children, Anna Siscoe, Mike Monroe, Judy Duke, and Randy Lepper were all investigated, released from custody, and cleared of all charges. Due to this and other court proceedings, the murder trial would not start until March 1966. All of the defendants were put on trial together, though they were all—aside from Ricky and Coy—represented by different lawyers.

Overseeing the case was Judge Saul Rabb. With over twenty years on the bench, Judge Rabb had gained a reputation for being tough but fair. Unwilling to delay the trial any further, he denied bail for all the defendants.

With six defendants and five lawyers, the trial would be a difficult one from the start. William C. Erbecker, Gertrude's lawyer, filed several preliminary pleadings in an effort to delay the court proceedings, much to Judge Rabb's annoyance.

Forrest Bowman, representing both Johnny Baniszewski and Coy Hubbard, tried to get the indictment against Johnny overturned due to his age. In Indiana, children under fifteen were considered incapable of criminal intent. Unfortunately for Bowman and his clients, this did not apply if there was enough evidence against the child. The law really only provided full protection from criminal prosecution to a child under seven.

The neighborhood children released from custody reappeared now as witnesses. Randy Lepper admitted that he saw Gertrude abuse Sylvia to the point where the girl cried "but no tears came out of her eyes." He also made mention of the incident with the soda bottle, which had prompted Stephanie to slap Sylvia.

Dr. Charles Ellis, having been called to testify for the prosecution, presented a diagram of a human torso which he used to illustrate the number and location of Sylvia's wounds. He had used colored pencils to draw on the diagram; purple was for bruises, red for burns and cuts, and green for "indeterminate" abrasions and lacerations. By the time he finished his statement, the torso was a brightly colored reflection of Sylvia's agony that was still not representative of everything she had endured. Ellis had simply run out of colors during his interview.

Eventually, the question on everyone's minds was put forward: Why didn't Sylvia fight back? Dr. Arthur Kebel said she must have been in too much shock, too weak to resist or try to escape. Where could she have gone anyway? Plus, everyone knew she would never leave Jenny behind.

As for Jenny, she faced a variety of cruel questions from Erbecker.

"You were perfectly free to go and tell anybody what you saw, weren't you?" he asked.

"Yes," Jenny admitted.

"You could have told the neighbors about this if you wanted to, couldn't you?" he went on.

"I could've," she said, starting to cry. "That don't mean I wanted to die, though."

"But you didn't, did you, Miss Likens?"

"No," she said sadly.

Next, James Nedeff, representing Ricky Hobbs, grilled Jenny. He mentioned that just days prior to Sylvia's death, John Baniszewski Sr. had come with the dog. "Your sister was in agony, had told you she was dying, she was sick and she was in the basement. Why did you not tell him?"

The defendants' lawyers scrutinized every move Jenny had made during her time with Gertrude. How could she allow all this to happen to her own sister?

It is a question that observers find themselves asking about this case, even decades later. There appears to be no grand, satisfactory answer.

Jenny was a scared, disabled child against a troop of tormentors. "I told you why I did not tell. Gertrude told me if I told anyone I would get the same treatment Sylvia was getting."

The tactic employed by all lawyers in court was to try and pin the blame on the other defendants. Notably, however, the best argument that William C. Erbecker, Gertrude's lawyer, could come up with was that she was simply insane.

However, proving such a claim would be no easy feat. Gertrude looked bad no matter which way he spun her story. She had either passively allowed this terrible crime to happen, or worse—she had been an active and willing participant, the ringleader behind it all, the one who struck the first blow and put it in the heads of her brood of children that this was something they could and should do as well.

It was certainly what most people seemed to think. Word about the crime had spread quickly in the local area, and many citizens were calling for Gertrude's head already. This was troubling. The law was supposed to be objective, and while public opinion was not supposed to affect the outcome of a trial, these kinds of biases tended to run deep. Erbecker was well aware that his client was already seen as the villain, and maybe it was for good reason, but it was his duty to make sure she got a fair trial anyway.

The case against his client was built rapidly as more witnesses testified, and not just for the prosecution's case. With this many defendants standing trial, it was expected that they would all turn on each other, but he had not anticipated that they would all point the finger at Gertrude so soon.

Erbecker lay out the argument: Gertrude outright denied her involvement. At most she would admit to giving both Sylvia and Jenny the occasional spanking as discipline, and that she had been given permission to do so by the girls' own father. But spankings were nothing. It was certainly not abnormal at that era in history, and the Likens girls had likely been struck by their own parents more times than they could count. They did not even curb Sylvia's bad behavior—and Sylvia was *bad*. One could not forget that. Her troublesome ways caused quite a lot of stress for Gertrude. Combine that with poverty, ill health, and the responsibility for caring for nine children, and it was enough to drive anyone crazy.

So, Gertrude had to be crazy. She simply had to have been to commit a crime of this magnitude. That was, *if* she had done it at all. That still needed to be proven beyond a reasonable doubt.

Still, most witnesses did not buy that Gertrude was legally insane. Included among them was a local psychologist named Jerome Joseph Relkin (notably, though he was a psychologist, he had not yet earned the credentials to be referred to as a doctor) who worked for the Beatty Memorial Hospital in Westville, Indiana, an institution for the criminally insane and was hired specifically by Erbecker. Relkin is possibly the most interesting witness to argue for Gertrude Baniszewski's defense.

Prior to his appearance in court, Relkin had interviewed Gertrude extensively, for around three hours, and performed different psychological exams. This included a "hand test." This test involved showing Gertrude various photos of hands and asking her to describe what she thought the hands were doing. The idea was that, based on her responses, Relkin could better assess her personality. In particular, he could determine whether or not she was a person prone to violence and aggression.

The specifics of the interview and exams are not known, though they were seemingly intense enough to leave Gertrude highly agitated, necessitating some time for her to cool off between each one.

Erbecker asked if the process left his client depressed.

"Oh, yes," Relkin answered. "She broke down and cried on many occasions."

Next, Erbecker asked if Relkin had reached a conclusion with these exams.

The psychologist responded with the following: "…she is a passive, dependent person. I would say generally not psychotic, has not any thinking disorder, knows right from wrong, but from her present personality, as I view it, I think it is highly consistent with her story of what happened in the basement was true."

Relkin was later asked what other opinions he had formed on the patient, and what he had to say about Gertrude was far from flattering: "...it is highly improbable she could be sophisticated enough to simulate or fool me on the test and the test data was very consistent with the interview data... [She is] very passive, dependent person and rather than being sadistic she is masochistic... She has a need to be punished herself, allow people to take advantage of her...

"She explained how her boyfriend beat her... And she still loves him, probably would still take him back, let him beat her up again too, if he would only give her a little bit of affection."

Relkin is, of course, referring to Dennis Wright Sr., the father of baby Dennis, and the younger man who Gertrude briefly "dated," the one who beat into having a miscarriage. He had long since washed his hands of her; now he was somewhere in West Germany, having been stationed there by the army. The child support he sent was even more sporadic than the little cash sent by John Sr. Everyone could tell that he had abandoned her for good—except, it seemed, for Gertrude herself.

Erbecker questions if someone so desperate for any sort of tenderness could also be cruel enough to beat a child. Relkin denied this, stating that Gertrude was the one more likely to be "stepped on all over."

Some of Relkin's comments may be shocking to the modern reader. He was essentially saying that Gertrude was simply too stupid, too weak-minded, and too much of a woman to have tortured Sylvia—but this was more or less the goal Erbecker had in mind: make his client appear too pathetic to have been a threat to anyone but herself.

Still, even if she hadn't been an active participant in the abuse, she had still been the adult in charge. She should have been somewhat liable for any harm done to a child in her care, even if she had not laid a single finger on them—and Sylvia had not merely been harmed. She had been tortured, mutilated, and the highest authority in the house had not done a single thing to stop it. This became a point of contention when Sylvia's tattooing was brought up. Was Gertrude aware that it was happening or not?

If Marie Baniszewski's testimony was to be believed, Gertrude helped Ricky get started and was then present for nearly the entire branding. When asked what her mother was doing for the rest of it, Marie said that her mother was "sitting down crocheting" in the front room.

How did she react to the end result? "She said that is a pretty good job," Marie clarified.

During previous court sessions, Gertrude had firmly denied knowing anything about it. Her claim was that she was quite sick at the time, unable to even get out of bed because she was so doped out of her mind on medication. If Sylvia had been screaming or crying, Gertrude was too loopy to have even heard her.

Here arose another problem. During her interviews with Relkin, Gertrude contradicted herself. The psychologist tried to elaborate: "She said she did know about the writing and at that time should have reported it to the police…. but in view of her personality structure, I feel that actually she was afraid to, she felt she would lose the love of the children—on which she so much depended."

Gertrude was a sad, sad woman—but was she insane?

Ultimately, Relkin decided that she was not, but she was not exactly mentally sound either: "…she expressed some doubts about the reality of the situation—in a way she can't believe this is all happening… In view of my evaluation of her current functioning I would accept her story, that under the stresses at that time she just withdrew and did not exercise the proper authority that she should have. She realizes this."

Erbecker did not allow Relkin to mention anything that may contradict the "character" being built in that courtroom. When Relkin brings up the topic of the sexual behavior of the other teenagers—including, alleged, "orgies" within the house—Erbecker emphasizes Gertrude's desperate need for love again: This was a woman who was so starved for attention and praise that she allowed anyone and everyone to take advantage of her: men, her own children, and the entire Likens family.

Indeed, Relkin brings the blame back around to Lester and Betty Likens. "It seems to me she was in no position to take care of more children. She had more than she could do to take care of her own, even with the small amount of money given her. Yet it seems people more or less pressured her into accepting the children. Perhaps she thought she might get attention and affection from these children she took; I don't know. She was sort of a pushover."

Sylvia became little more than a footnote of Gertrude's pathetic story during Relkin's testimony. He claims to believe Gertrude's version of events, placing him squarely in the minority of public opinion. He doubts that Gertrude had any dislike of the girl at all. "She said Sylvia had a right to live as much as any other girl," he recounted. "She felt guilty about not taking proper action. She felt if she had it might have prevented Sylvia's death. At the time she was too overwhelmed to be able to do anything about it and I don't think she realized fully at the time Sylvia would die."

It is no surprise that very few people found this last statement credible. The jury would come to find that Gertrude was not insane. She was maniacal, cruel, and bitter, but she was not insane. Her mistreatment of Sylvia, cold and so often calculating, proved so. She planned her torture out, and she took steps to protect herself from the consequences.

Gertrude was found guilty of first-degree murder. Paula, of second-degree. Both were sentenced to life in prison. Johnny, Ricky, and Coy were found guilty of manslaughter and would go on to serve less than two years in a state reformatory. John Hammond, who represented Stephanie, managed to prove his client's minimal involvement and got her charges dropped.

It was a sensational case that would go down as one of the worst in Indiana's history. Perhaps the only bright spot in this entire sad tale came once the trial ended and the tormentors were at last put away; Leroy New, the case's prosecutor, informally adopted Jenny.

She spent the rest of her youth in New's big house, making happy memories with his two daughters. For the first time, Jenny found stability, and her future was looking brighter than it ever had.

Still, there was a heaviness in her spirit that she knew could never heal. She would feel her sister's absence for the rest of her life.

"I just wish…" she would say. "That me and Sylvia could have been left with nice people like this, instead of with Gertrude."

Conclusion

THE SYLVIA LIKENS CASE IS AS SAD AS IT IS infuriating. Reading these grim details presents us, time and time again, with the fact that this unfortunate, blameless girl did not have to die. So many opportunities arose for her to be saved, but none were taken. Why? The answer to that question is complicated, but perhaps the simplest answer is that some people are just unlucky.

Indeed, many of the people involved were unlucky people. They were poor, uneducated, and surrounded by people who did not have their best interests in mind. As it turns out, tragedy would follow the Likens well after the death of their beloved daughter and sister.

Unable to cope, Lester and Betty would finally separate for good in 1967. Betty would die in 1999 at the age of seventy-one. Jenny's twin, Benny, would die that same year, aged forty-nine. He had since become an isolated schizophrenic, and his remaining family only found out about his death when letters addressed to him were sent back with the word "DECEASED" stamped on them.

Jenny, who got married less than five years after the trial and had two children, developed long-lasting anxiety issues. In a 2018 interview by *The Claremont Sun*, Dianna confirmed that her youngest sister never got over what happened in 1965.

"…at times she had breakdowns. She had to go on nerve pills for the rest of her life. But I wasn't living close to her since I lived out of state. But I know that she had very bad memories. Bless her heart. She just didn't talk about it. I guess it was hard to deal with. Of course, I understand that it would be for anybody." Jenny died from a heart attack in 2004 at only fifty-four.

Lester Cecil Likens would die in 2013 at the age of eighty-six. Like Jenny, he was never able to shake off the guilt despite his daughter's belief that he and Betty were guilty of being too trusting. The fate of Danny is uncertain. He was last heard from in 2004.

The only Likens still believed to be alive at the time of this writing is Dianna, now named Dianna Bedwell. In May 2015, she and her husband, Cecil Knutson, went missing in a remote area of the southern California desert after a wrong turn stranded their vehicle. They were found two weeks later, Dianna barely clinging to life, her husband deceased. She later told reporters that she had survived off of oranges and rainwater.

Ricky Hobbs died young. Less than four years after his release from Indiana Reformatory in 1968, he developed an aggressive form of lung cancer, and also allegedly suffered an unspecified mental illness. He passed away on January 2, 1972, at the age of twenty-one.

Coy Hubbard, also released in 1968, remained in the state and turned to a life of crime. In 1977, he was charged with the murders of two men but was ultimately acquitted. He died in 2007 at the age of fifty-six.

Johnny changed his name to John Blake and became a minister and children's counselor. He died in 2005 at the age of fifty-two.

Stephanie Baniszewski was the only one of Gertrude's older children to avoid incarceration. After the dust of the trial settled, she changed her name and continued her education, ultimately becoming a teacher in another state.

In a controversial decision, the Indiana Supreme Court overturned both Gertrude and Paula's convictions on the basis that the negative publicity surrounding the case made it impossible for mother and daughter to have gotten a fair trial at the time. In 1971, Paula pleaded guilty to voluntary manslaughter and was sentenced to two to twenty years for her role in Sylvia's death. Incredibly, despite having attempted to escape prison twice, Paula was released on parole in 1972. She married, changed her name to Paula Pace, and moved to Iowa.

In 1998, she was hired by a school district in the city of Conrad. She began as a custodian but later became a teacher's aide. She worked with special needs students and was, as far as anyone in her new life knew, normal, hardworking, and kind. This image of her was shattered in 2012 when an anonymous Facebook user informed Conrad locals as well as the police. She was soon fired when the school board realized she had lied on her job application.

Then there's Gertrude.

Following the 1971 retrial, Gertrude Baniszewski was again convicted of first-degree murder. She spent the next fourteen years in the Indiana's Women's Prison. She was said to have been a model prisoner, worked as a seamstress in the prison's shop, and was a born-again Christian. Other inmates, particularly the younger among them, were fond of her and called her "Mom." When the question of Gertrude ever receiving parole came up, her prison friends became some of her most vocal supporters, believing that she had truly changed.

Despite public outcry (including a petition to keep her in prison for life that received over forty thousand signatures), Gertrude was ultimately granted parole in 1985. She changed her name to Nadine Van Fossan and moved in with Paula's family in Iowa. She continued to minimize her involvement in Sylvia Likens's death until her death from lung cancer in 1990. She was sixty-one.

The news of her passing was reported in a newspaper obituary that happened to be read by Jenny. She clipped it and mailed the section to her mother with an accompanying note: "Some good news. Damn old Gertrude died. Ha ha ha! I am happy about that."

The murder of Sylvia Likens continues to haunt the American Midwest. The tragedy and its aftermath continue to be subject to discussions about crime and justice. What do we make about the people at its center?

Even Gertrude, who was the ringleader of it all, was undeniably an unfortunate woman. In any case, she baffled everyone. Here was a woman with no history of violent behavior who became a sadistic torture killer. How did it happen?

Somehow, the idea that she was simply jealous and hateful feels unsatisfying. Not only that, it worries us. How many Gertrude Baniszewskis are walking among us today with the only thing separating them from evil is a minuscule degree of power?

We can only learn from the mistakes of the past.

References

"House of Horrors," Retrieved from:
https://malefactorsregister.com/wp/house-of-horrors/

"Murder of Sylvia Likens," Retrieved from:
https://en.wikipedia.org/wiki/Murder_of_Sylvia_Likens

"Gertrude Baniszewski" Retrieved from:
https://murderpedia.org/female.B/b/baniszewski.htm

"The Murder of Sylvia Likens 50 Years Later," Retrieved from:
https://www.indianapolismonthly.com/longform/likens-looking-back-indianas-infamous-crime-50-years-later

"'Torture Mother' – Gertrude Baniszewski," Retrieved from:
https://www.scribd.com/podcast/418981856/Torture-Mother-Gertrude-Baniszewski-In-the-summer-of-1965-in-Indiana-teenagers-Sylvia-and-Jenny-Likens-were-invited-to-stay-in-the-home-of-their

Green, R. (2018) *Torture Mom: A Chilling True Story of Confinement, Mutilation and Murder* Ryan Green Publishing

Dean, J. (2008) *House of Evil: The Indiana Torture Slaying* St. Martin's Paperbacks

Millett, K. (1979) *The Basement: Meditations on a Human Sacrifice* Simon and Schuster

Acknowledgements

This is a special thanks to the following readers who have taken time out of their busy schedule to be part of True Crime Seven Team. Thank you all so much for all the feedbacks and support!

James.

Sherry Quimby, Andrew Ayers, Shelley Specht, Kris Bowers, Sherry Whitaker, Sharron Henry, Robert Upton, Liberty Susan Gabor, Angie Gratton, Amanda, Alan Kleynenberg, Alicia Gephart, Alicia Gir, Richard Allen, Alma Verster, Datrice St.Denis, Anna McCown, April Clarke, Jennifer Hanlon, Ashlynn Stinson, Alea Slocomb, Angela Brockman, Maryann Quinn, Bambi Dawn Goggio, Casey Renee Bates, Kurt Brown, Beth Alfreit, Lee Fowley, Shelli Blankenbaker, Amanda, Barbara English, Bruce Weldin, Bryce Hartford, Brooke Youngs, Chad Mellor, Cara Butcher, Joyce Carroll, Allyssa Howells, Cory Lindsey, Clara Cortes, Nancy Harrison, Carrie Roberson, Joan Baker, Connie White, Dawn Winter, David Edmonds, David Helling, Dani Bigner, Awilda Roman, Donna Champion, Donna Freile, Betty May, Rebecca Donnell, Patti Kelley, Emma Futter, Marion E. M. Newman, Francis Bernardi, Larry J. Field, Linda J Evans, Diane Kourajian, Cathy Russell, Helaine Lasky, Deborah Hanson, Shannon Bruce, Toni Marie Rinella, Jessica Harvey, Huw, Angela Sims, John Edward, Ray Verrett, Jessica Bowman, Jennifer Fail, Jennie, Jo Pardoe, Wanda Jones, Jon Wiederhorn, James, Jeanine Copperstone, Judy Stephens, Laura Rouston, Laura Mish, Lissette Ortiz, Landa-Lou Goodridge, Justine, Fran Joyner, Karin Dennis, Karen A. McCabe, Kay, Jennifer Jones, Kelly Wise, Dezirae, Chandra, Michelle Simpson, Deirdre Green, Debbie Hill, Lorrie VanMeter, Leslie Rasmussen, Kimberly Herout, Sue Reutzel, Maguelonne, Marquita Leggett, Jason, Miranda Sowers, Wanda L. Michele Gosselin, Barbara Pollock, Melody Sanderson, Monica Yokel, Marcia Heacock, Underwood, Rebecca Stallman Catazaro, Jason C. Tillery, Muhammad Nizam Bin Mohtar, Tamara, Bontnie Kernene, Beverly Harris, Natalie Gwinn, Natasha Rachel B, Hoadley, Cynthia Z. Miller, Nicky McLean, Jamie Rasmussen, Sue Wallace, Ole Pedersen, Keri Wallace, Kathy Morgan, Patricia Oliver, Amanda Gallegos, Cheryl Griffis, Paula Jackson, Lisa Bogenschneider, Stacia Lanway, Robert Fritsch, Christy Riemenschneider, Shane Neely, Lynn Butler, Rebecca Ednie, Susan Weaver, Brenda M Bennett, Ferne Miller, Tammy Sitlinger, Tamela L. Matuska, Don Price, Caric Boghozian, Tina Bullard, Dansel Thaakirah Wolfe Charles, Thomm Stewart Rae, Tina Shattuck, Marcie Walters, Brandy Noble, Tara Pendley, Jan Tweed,

Lee Barta,

161

Continue Your Exploration Into

The Murderous Minds

Excerpt From True Crime Explicit Volume 10

I
The Abduction

YOU NEVER THINK IT WILL HAPPEN TO YOU.

Countless people love true crime. They love the mystery, the drama, and all the gory details. For many, true crime is little more than grim entertainment, but for some unlucky few, the pain is very, very real.

In 1985, Lexington County, part of Columbia, South Carolina, was a quiet community. Most people knew each other. Churchgoers formed strong, tight-knit communities. Within that group were the Smiths, an average, unassuming family with two beautiful daughters.

Murder, kidnapping—it was the kind of stuff that only happened in movies. No one could have ever anticipated that one of the girls would become the victim of a crime.

It was a sweltering hot day, over one hundred degrees, when Sharon "Shari" Faye Smith was taken. The date was May 31, 1985, the tail-end of spring, but living in Southern Carolina meant that summer came early. In spite of the heat, Shari had had a busy day. With her high school graduation just two days away, followed by a class trip to the Bahamas, she found herself busy preparing for a new stage of life. She had spent the morning doing the daily prayer she always shared with her family before heading off to rehearse with her chorus teacher, as she had been selected to sing "The Star-Spangled Banner" at the commencement ceremony alongside a classmate. After a much-needed pool party at a friend's house, she was more than ready to head home for the day.

She had no idea that, within a tiny, seemingly insignificant window of time, an unknown predator had already set his sights on her.

Still clad in her swimsuit, she drove her blue Chevette to the Smith family home located at 5700 Platt Springs Road of Lexington, a suburb of the state's capitol city. The house had been built in the center of a vast plot of land, leaving all four sides surrounded by what was, at this time of year, a sea of drying grass save for the swimming pool in the back. The pathway from the mailbox to the front door was around seven hundred feet, but it was a distance Shari had grown used to crossing.

Before she did so again, however, she needed to check the mail.

Shari opened the mailbox and took out a few letters. She hardly had the chance to look at them when she heard a car pull up behind her. A man she did not recognize looked at her with hungry eyes from the driver's seat. He said something she could not hear over the sound of both cars' engines still running.

The man did not bother to repeat himself. Instead, he hurried out of the car, closing the space between him and Shari in the blink of an eye. He grabbed her, and to Shari's horror, pressed what she soon realized was the cold metal barrel of a gun to her body. If she wanted to live, he warned her, then she better get in his car.

Shari had a righteous upbringing and had been raised to see the best in everyone. In all her innocence, she likely had no idea what fate awaited her when she stepped into the car. When he drove off, did she understand that she would never return?

But what is known for certain is that her father Bob Smith, a Baptist pastor and engineer, had been the first person to notice that something was amiss. He and his wife, Hilda, had been out back by the pool around the time their daughter arrived. When he first saw her car parked at the end of their driveway, he had assumed she had merely stopped to pick up the mail. When he looked out the window a while later, however, he saw the car still there, unmoved. Hilda tried to soothe his worries by offering the possibility that Shari was reading a letter sent by Dawn, the eldest Smith sister, and got caught up because the two were very close, but a sinking feeling came over him.

Bob hurried outside to his own car and drove down to check on his daughter. His worst fears were realized.

Shari was gone. Her car was running and all her belongings, including her shoes, were still inside. A handful of letters were strewn across the ground, indicating that she had dropped them suddenly, and perhaps unwillingly. He could make out her bare footprints leading away from the front seat, but none were leading back. Worst of all was what he found in her purse: her medication.

Shari Faye suffered from a rare medical condition: diabetes insipidus, more commonly known as "water diabetes." It meant that Shari's body had a hard time regulating fluids and could quickly become dehydrated, something that, given the intense heat, could quickly put her in serious danger without her medicine.

Panicked, Pastor Smith hurried back inside the house to get to Hilda. He told his wife that her car had still been running but she was not in it.

Mrs. Smith was understandably just as worried. While her husband called the police, she hopped into her own car and drove around in search of Shari. It pained her to have to return to the house without her and endure the half-hour wait before help arrived. All Hilda could do at the moment was pace around the property, praying silently for her daughter's safety.

In South Carolina today, there is no amount of time required before a family can report a person missing. This was unfortunately not the case for many states in previous decades. Had Shari been anyone else, it is likely the authorities would have needed to wait before beginning their search, considering the fact that she was right on the brink of adulthood. The fact that Shari was a diabetic without her medicine, however, created a sense of urgency that got police to act right away. What followed was one of the largest searches conducted in the history of Lexington County.

Air teams were called in to conduct aerial searches. The governor's office's Emergency Preparedness Division arrived to set up tractor-trailer's that would serve as a base for the investigation. These trailers were full of all sorts of equipment, including telephones, radios, and cameras, that could keep the place running twenty-four hours a day.

Authorities were eager to help not just because of the urgency of Shari's health needs, but also because they were already familiar enough with the Smiths to know it was unlike the girl to have run away.

"She's not a runaway," Captain Bob Ford of the sheriff's department told the press. "We can't accept any theories that she ran away from home."

The efforts were led by Lexington County Sheriff James R. Metts, who also set up base in a trailer near the Smith home. The plan was for this place to remain accessible at all hours in case any new information regarding Shari or her abductor came in. Having everything in one place meant that they could save precious time—Shari's time.

They would need the public's help. Whenever something strange happened in a small town, word got around fast. Soon after, calls came in from locals reporting sightings of suspicious vehicles. Two men who had driven past the Platt Springs Road just after three in the afternoon claimed to have seen Shari standing at the mailbox. At the same time, a car, described as being reddish-purple or maroon in color, was coming up the opposite side of the road, headed directly towards the Smith home. Based off of their brief sighting, the men believed the other vehicle to be an Oldsmobile Cutlass, possibly a model from 1982 to 1984. The driver appeared to be a man in his thirties.

When they passed by, they looked in their rear-view mirror. The taillights of the Oldsmobile came on. The vehicle had come to a stop at the mailbox.

A short while later, the two men passed by the Smith home again. This time, they saw Shari's Chevette, but they did not see Shari.

With no luck that first day, the search carried on into the weekend, expanding to over a hundred volunteers combing the area, undaunted by the heat. Helicopters and bloodhounds were used. The phone at the Smith family house was wiretapped. Still, no progress was made aside from the recovery of a red bandanna belonging to Shari. It was located on the side of the road less than a mile from the house, and law enforcement believed that she may have dropped it from a moving vehicle, a sort of breadcrumb in her kidnapper's path, but unfortunately it did not lead to further clues.

It had been a long and hard day. They had combed through about twenty miles of land with almost nothing to show for it. At least two volunteers fainted from heat exhaustion. Another man stepped on a nail while a police officer suffered a nasty spider bite. They were all taken to the Lexington County Hospital by an ambulance that had been kept at the scene in case of emergencies.

When the search concluded for the day just before six in the evening, the temperature still hovered over ninety-seven degrees. Everyone was in need of rest, though the Sheriff asked them to return early the next morning before the worst of the heat.

Past experience with similar crimes led the South Carolina Law Enforcement Division (commonly abbreviated as SLED in sources) to expect a ransom demand to come in soon. As grim as the prospect that Shari was being held for ransom was, it was actually the preferable situation than most alternatives, because ransom demands meant the perp was likely to communicate with law enforcement and being able to communicate with a perp made it easier to catch them. It also meant it would have been more likely that Shari would have been kept alive as a bargaining chip—that is, if they were lucky. When the third day came with no demand, the local authorities were unsure what to do next.

It was clear that this was no ordinary case. It was something bigger than their resources could handle on their own, so they needed help.

The End of **The Preview**

Visit us at **truecrimeseven.com** or **scan QR Code using your phone's camera app** to find more true crime books and other cool goodies.

About True Crime Seven

True Crime Seven is about exploring the stories of the sinful minds in this world. From unknown murderers to well-known serial killers.

Our writers come from all walks of life but with one thing in common and that is they are all true crime enthusiasts. You can learn more about them below:

Ryan Becker is a True Crime author who started his writing journey in late 2016. Like most of you, he loves to explore the process of how individuals turn their darkest fantasies into a reality. Ryan has always had a passion for storytelling. So, writing is the best output for him to combine his fascination with psychology and true crime. It is Ryan's goal for his readers to experience the full immersion with the dark reality of the world just like how he used to do it in his younger days.

Nancy Alyssa Veysey is a writer and author of true crime books, including the bestselling, Mary Flora Bell: The Horrific True Story Behind an Innocent Girl Serial Killer. Her medical degree and work in the field of forensic psychology, along with postgraduate studies in criminal justice, criminology and pre-law, allow her to bring a unique perspective to her writing.

Kurtis-Giles Veysey is a young writer who began his writing career in the fantasy genre. In late 2018, he has parlayed his love and knowledge of history into writing nonfiction accounts of true crime stories which occurred in centuries past. Told from a historical perspective, Kurtis-Giles brings these victims and their killers back to life with vivid descriptions of these heinous crimes.

Kelly Gaines is a writer from Philadelphia. Her passion for storytelling began in childhood and carried into her college career. She received a B.A. in English from Saint Joseph's University in 2016 with a concentration in Writing Studies. Now part of the real world, Kelly enjoys comic books, history documentaries, and a good scary story. In her true crime work, Kelly focuses on the motivations of the killers and backgrounds of the victims to draw a more complete picture of each individual. She deeply enjoys writing for True Crime Seven and looks forward to bringing more spine-tingling tales to readers.

James Parker the pen-name of a young writer from New Jersey who started his writing journey with play-writing. He has always been fascinated with the psychology of murderers and how the media might play a role in their creation. James loves to constantly test out new styles and ideas in his writing so one day he can find something cool and unique to himself.

Brenda Brown is a writer and an illustrator-cartoonist. Her art can be found in books distributed both nationally and internationally. She has also written many books related to her graduate degree in psychology and her minor in history. Like many true crime enthusiasts, she loves exploring the minds of those who see the world as a playground for expressing the darker side of themselves—the side that people usually locked up and hid from scrutiny.

Genoveva Ortiz is a Los Angeles-based writer who began her career writing scary stories while still in college. After receiving a B.A. in English in 2018, she shifted her focus to nonfiction and the real-life horrors of crime and unsolved mysteries. Together with True Crime Seven, she is excited to further explore the world of true crime through a social justice perspective.

You can learn more about us and our writers at:

truecrimeseven.com/about

Get our **Bestseller for FREE on Audible** when you sign up to Audible for a free 30-Day Trial. You can cancel at any time if you don't like the experience of listening on the go. But you can keep your free book.

Sign up at: **https://geni.us/A1ce8iC**

Or **scan QR Code using your phone's camera app.**

Listen to 48 True Crime Stories Today For FREE.

For updates about new releases, as well as exclusive promotions, join True Crime Seven readers' group and you can also **receive a free book today.** Thank you and see you soon.
Sign up at: **freebook.truecrimeseven.com/**

Or **scan QR Code using your phone's camera app.**

Dark Fantasies Turned Reality

Prepare yourself, we're not going to **hold back on details or cut out any of the gruesome truths...**

Printed in Dunstable, United Kingdom